A Guide to Impactful
Teacher Evaluations

What if everything we thought we knew about effective teacher evaluations was wrong? *A Guide to Impactful Teacher Evaluations* walks educators through an important shift in thinking about how to evaluate teachers: from systems focused on individuals and results to solutions focused on collectives and processes.

Disregarding older, ineffective models that rely on faulty assumptions, this book embraces new approaches for measuring teacher competency that achieve valid assessment of effective teaching, teacher professional growth, and student learning. Chapters explore teacher evaluation systems based on professional learning community principles, confront the current system of teacher evaluation that has led to frustration, criticism, and disrespect, provide strategies for delivering new skills and supporting teachers' growth, and include "Tips and Talking Points" for schools and districts.

Outlining best practice and sharing actionable tools grounded in collaboration and teamwork, this book helps K-12 school leaders explore teacher evaluation that has a real and lasting impact on the profession and student learning.

Joseph O. Rodgers has experience leading urban and rural schools, as well as at the district level. He is the CEO of the Center for Collective Efficacy.

Other Eye On Education Books Available from Routledge
(www.routledge.com/eyeoneducation)

A Guide to Early College and Dual Enrollment Programs: Designing and Implementing Programs for Student Achievement
Russ Olwell

The Strategy Playbook for Educational Leaders: Principles and Processes
Isobel Stevenson and Jennie Weiner

Unpacking Your Learning Targets: Aligning Student Learning to Standards
Sean McWherter

Strategic Talent Leadership for Educators: A Practical Toolkit
Amy A. Holcombe

Becoming a Transformative Leader: A Guide to Creating Equitable Schools
Carolyn M. Shields

Bringing Innovative Practices to Your School: Lessons from International Schools
Jayson W. Richardson

Working with Students that Have Anxiety: Creative Connections and Practical Strategies
Beverley H. Johns, Donalyn Heise, and Adrienne D. Hunter

Implicit Bias in Schools: A Practitioner's Guide
Gina Laura Gullo, Kelly Capatosto, and Cheryl Staats

Leadership in America's Best Urban Schools
Joseph F. Johnson, Jr, Cynthia L. Uline, and Lynne G. Perez

Leading Learning for ELL Students: Strategies for Success
Catherine Beck and Heidi Pace

A Guide to Impactful Teacher Evaluations

Let's Finally Get It Right!

Joseph O. Rodgers

Routledge
Taylor & Francis Group

NEW YORK AND LONDON

First published 2021
by Routledge
52 Vanderbilt Avenue, New York, NY 10017

and by Routledge
2 Park Square, Milton Park, Abingdon, Oxon OX14 4RN

Routledge is an imprint of the Taylor & Francis Group, an informa business

Library of Congress Cataloging-in-Publication Data
Names: Rodgers, Joseph O., author.
Title: A guide to impactful teacher evaluations: let's finally
get it right!/Joseph O. Rodgers.
Identifiers: LCCN 2020043865 (print) | LCCN 2020043866 (ebook) |
ISBN 9780367611484 (hardback) | ISBN 9780367611491 (paperback) |
ISBN 9781003104353 (ebook)
Subjects: LCSH: Teachers–Rating of. | Professional learning communities.
Classification: LCC LB2838 .R64 2021 (print) | LCC LB2838 (ebook) |
DDC 371.14/4–dc23
LC record available at https://lccn.loc.gov/2020043865
LC ebook record available at https://lccn.loc.gov/2020043866

ISBN: 978-0-367-61148-4 (hbk)
ISBN: 978-0-367-61149-1 (pbk)
ISBN: 978-1-003-10435-3 (ebk)

Typeset in Optima
by Newgen Publishing UK

Access the eResources: www.routledge.com/9780367611491

Contents

List of Figures		vi
Meet the Author		vii
Preface		ix
eResources		xiv

1.	**Historical and Conceptual Background Knowledge**	1
2.	**Current Teacher Evaluations Systems Overview**	23
3.	**Faulty Assumptions**	43
4.	**Teacher Quality, Effectiveness and Evaluation**	68
5.	**Dawn is Here: A New Day for Educators**	98
6.	**Learning Evaluation System**	118

Figures

1.1	Key texts in teacher evaluation history	18
2.1	Teacher evaluation theory	35
4.1	Student-centered observation rubric	88
4.2	Student engagement	89
4.3	Student purpose	90
4.4	Student productivity	91
4.5	Student collaboration	92
4.6	Positive relationships	93
5.1	Broad assumptions of teacher efficacy	99
5.2	Assumptions comparison	109
5.3	The four Cs of a Learning Evaluation	115
6.1	Theory of action	119
6.2	Teacher evaluation emphasis comparison	121
6.3	Learning Evaluation assumptions	122
6.4	Learning Evaluation 1	123
6.5	Learning Evaluation 2	124
6.6	Learning Evaluation rubric assumptions guide	141
6.7	Learning assumptions concept flow	142
6.8	Assumptions of a Learning Evaluation	143
6.9	Broad assumptions of teacher efficacy	144
6.10	Paramount assumption	144
6.11	Professional learning communities	144
6.12	Mission and beliefs	144
6.13	Professional learning communities: graphic	145
6.14	Contributions to learning and knowledge	145

Meet the Author

Dr. Joseph Rodgers has experience as a teacher, middle school basketball coach, elementary and middle school administrator and Title 1 program director. He has served in urban and rural schools. He is a graduate of the University of West Georgia's doctorate in School Improvement in the department of Leadership, Research and School Improvement. In his spare time, he leads the Center for Collective Efficacy (www.collective-efficacy.com), researching, writing and assisting schools with strategic planning.

Preface

"Ideas have consequences" (Weaver, 1948): and bad ideas have bad consequences. Evaluating teachers as we currently do was a bad idea, with negatively impactful consequences. Our country's diversity is its greatest strength. We need to free educators in this country to serve students and families like they never have before. It starts with our processes, and ensuring we are not only doing the right things but doing them the right way.

Schools, school districts, state agencies and even the federal government have weighed in on teacher evaluation policy to assess the nation's teacher workforce. None has been successful, and teacher evaluation remains a highly debated, contested and adversarial point of emphasis for stakeholders, professionals, researchers, policymakers and lawmakers. Why? Why has the debate and implementation of effective teacher evaluation systems failed on many levels, and why does it remain in a state of ambiguity, frustration and ineffectiveness?

The problem with past and current teacher evaluation systems, tools, mechanisms and philosophies is the false assumptions that have guided teacher evaluations for years. The foundational faulty assumptions about what effective teaching is and how it should be assessed have stifled the professional growth of teachers and inhibited student growth and achievement. Until educators and policymakers change their thinking and start with the correct assumptions, teacher evaluation systems will never accomplish their intended purpose: valid assessment of effective teaching, teacher professional growth and, most importantly, student learning.

Currently, schools across the country use a patchwork of different methods to evaluate teachers. These systems differ dramatically in what evaluators must record—as if there were no established consensus on what's most important to good teaching. Some are so complex and time-consuming that educators struggle to complete them. And despite their differences, they're all grounded in a few assumptions: that good teaching is a matter of individual achievement, completing a series of specified tasks or behaviors is how teachers become effective, principal observations and feedback lead to improvement and teacher quality can be evaluated objectively. All of these assumptions, and many more, are false.

We don't have to rely on this scattershot, unscientific approach. A robust and well-done body of work exists on performance evaluations and organizational psychology, showing that excellent job performance springs from building an effective organizational culture and creating processes that help people collaborate to learn new skills, inquire, solve problems and help each other be better at their jobs. Our profession could use this knowledge to boost the effectiveness of teachers, schools and entire districts. It's just that the insights from this research aren't being used to create teacher evaluations, confusing norms and conflicting objectives. As long as educators build teacher evaluation systems on erroneous foundations, they will find themselves in a never-ending cycle of frustration, criticism, disrespect and public scrutiny.

It's time for a fundamental shift in philosophy. *A Guide to Impactful Teacher Evaluations: Let's Finally Get It Right!* is the shift in thinking educators are longing for.

Currently, with the passage of the Every Student Succeeds Act, states once again have the freedom to create and evaluate teachers with systems of their own choosing. If only we could change the assumptions that dictate educators' behavior and policymakers' thinking, the nation's students would finally have a chance to see unprecedented learning and achievement.

To my knowledge, this is an original work in the context of education. I have consulted studies and books from a wealth of fields, looking at the issues of teacher evaluation from multiple angles. The results of my research lead me to propose a dramatic shift—from systems focused on individuals and results to ones focused on collectives and processes.

This is a theory of action. The construct presented in this book needs to be implemented, studied and refined. I hope this book stirs the conversation enough so that the construct can receive the attention it needs. We've tried what doesn't work—let's finally get it right!

How This Book is Organized

Teacher evaluations in the United States have been in constant flux for decades. There is a considerable amount of research seeking to measure teaching quality, with mixed and often unconclusive reviews. This book explores research into performance appraisals from various domains and teacher evaluations through the years. The later chapters explore teacher evaluation through a series of lenses, offering discussion of research, tips and talking points, case studies (which are fictional, based on general experience and observations of other educators), tools, rubrics and graphics, to guide the discussion around teacher evaluations. Chapter 6 culminates with an example of a new way to evaluate teachers, a Learning Evaluation.

 # Chapter 1: Historical and Conceptual Background Knowledge

This book starts with the idea of performance appraisals and evaluations of employees. A proper understanding of this concept is important for educators trying to conceptualize and realize the need for change in our current educational systems. Consulting research from multiple sectors of our society and economy, we find that performance appraisals and evaluation of employees receive very dismal reviews. Education is not immune to those challenges.

 # Chapter 2: Current Teacher Evaluations Systems Overview

The second chapter focuses on our current models, post-Race to the Top (RTT) legislation. State documents are consulted and critiqued. It is important to note that the problem of teacher evaluations is not limited to a single state or region. It has been proven that teacher evaluations have had an inadequate impact, even in terms of their own conflicting purposes and objectives, for decades in nearly every state. This is not a new problem, and every state has struggled with its own unique challenges. This chapter reviews various models, methods and theories, and asks the question (in "Tips and Talking Points"): "If we continue current practices, will we have enough people that want to be educators?"

Chapter 3: Faulty Assumptions

Teacher evaluations have little impact on the education profession. The foundation of the entire system is built on faulty assumptions. Unless we can state those assumptions explicitly and re-write them, teacher evaluations will continue to lack the impact needed to move the profession forward and improve schools.

Chapter 4: Teacher Quality, Effectiveness and Evaluation

We need a new definition of quality teaching. The metrical way of assessing teacher effectiveness has not proven to be an effective method. Once we have a new definition of quality teaching, new assumptions can be built, for a more robust and professional system. The new definition of teaching will require a new lens through which to view quality teaching. A Student-Centered Observation Rubric is presented at the end of this chapter, as a new perspective that explicitly uses the actions and behaviors of the students to assess teaching quality.

Chapter 5: Dawn is Here: A New Day for Educators

New assumptions are discussed and conceptualized through the new definition of quality teaching. Without new, explicitly stated assumptions, teacher evaluations, and in particular the four Cs of a Learning Evaluation that I propose, can never be apprehended. A new system needs to be built, on new assumptions, based on what we already know about student learning, the practice of quality teaching and collaboration.

Chapter 6: Learning Evaluation System

In Chapter 6, a Learning Evaluation for teachers is set out. The system is purposefully subjective and requires local school collaboration to implement. Each component is also based on its own set of new assumptions. The documents used in this system are free, and open to addition or subtraction. Chapter 6 culminates with a rubric, guides, tables and graphics as resources any school can use to create an impactful Learning Evaluation for teachers.

References

Weaver, R. M. (1948). *Ideas have consequences*. Chicago, IL: University of Chicago Press.

eResources

The resources listed below can be downloaded, printed, used to copy/paste text and/or manipulated to suit your own individualized use. You can access these downloads by visiting the book product page on our website: www.routledge.com/9780367611491. Click on the tab that reads "Support Material" and then select the file(s) you need.

Tool   Page

- Figure 5.3: The Four Cs of a Learning Evaluation   115
- Figure 6.4: Learning Evaluation 1   123
- Figure 6.5: Learning Evaluation 2   124
- Figure 6.8: Assumptions of a Learning Evaluation   143

Historical and Conceptual Background Knowledge

An understanding of the historical and conceptual background knowledge of performance appraisals is imperative to understanding teacher evaluation policy, implementation and consequences in the United States. The teacher evaluation policies that apply in the United States did not originate in the education field. Teacher evaluations in the United States and across the globe are modeled after the performance appraisal systems of the private sector. Studies and research in the area of performance appraisals have yielded very mixed reviews. In the literature there is a host of issues surrounding the concept, philosophy, management, implementation and unintended consequences of performance appraisals. Organizational psychologists, management and business experts and researchers alike have reviewed the findings of performance appraisals and are not sure of the best direction for the construct moving forward.

The concept of performance appraisals has made its way into every sector of our society. Researchers have repeatedly reached the conclusion that they are not living up to their intended consequences and may actually do more harm than good in moving an organization forward.

There are no quick fixes in the realm of performance appraisals. It is important that educational administrators understand the history of performance appraisals to better combat the problems facing our principals and teachers today. Without a proper understanding of performance appraisals, educators will find themselves in an endless loop of sincere intentions, broken systems and unintended consequences.

In this book, I will use terms such as performance appraisals, assessments, evaluations and judgements as synonymous when applying them to the current concept of teacher evaluations. They all reference the same con-cept: the judgement of an employee's performance.

Performance Appraisals

Performance appraisals have existed in almost every sector of our society for decades. In all their forms, they seek to measure how an employee is functioning in his or her job. Coens and Jenkins (2000) described the per-formance appraisal as

> a mandated process in which, for a specified period of time, all or a group of employees' work performance, behaviors, or traits are individually rated, judged, or described by a person other than the rated employee and the results are kept by the organization.

(p. 15)

Office managers, mail carriers, teachers, police officers, union stewards, salespersons—almost everyone who has a professional job has under-gone the performance review process. "Performance appraisal is a formal, summative process of evaluating job performance that has important consequences for individuals and organizations" (Murphy, Cleveland & Hanscom., 2018, p.17).

Performance assessments are ingrained in our way of life. From the time we were young, whether in school, on the basketball court, or auditioning for a play, someone, somewhere was keeping track and formally judging our performance. We have always had to make the grade, get the score or check off the box. As we grow older and enter the workforce, it is second nature to go through a performance review process. We have actually become pretty good at the process of giving the assessment and receiving the feedback, and even manipulating the results (Coens and Jenkins, 2000).

The modern history of performance review started in World War I, when the U.S. military created a metric rating system to identify poor performers. The practice caught on; recruits continued to be ranked during World War II, and by the 1940s 60% of U.S. companies used perform-ance reviews to determine bonuses and promotions. Peter Cappelli and Anna Tavis gave a straightforward history of performance reviews in their article "The performance management revolution" (2016), featured in the *Harvard Business Review.*

- 1950s: Douglas McGregor encourages assessments and goal setting
- 1960s: General Electric (GE) emphasizes accountability and growth
- 1970s: Objective merit-pay and accountability
- 1980s: GE reward top performers, accommodate the middle and get rid of the bottom performers
- 1990s: Assessment and rewards for top performers
- 2000s: Increase in direct reports for managers institutes time constraints
- 2011: Kelly Services abandons annual performance reviews
- 2012: Adobe eliminates annual performance reviews
- 2016: Deloitte, PwC and more embrace development feedback

What are institutions trying to achieve when they do this? Performance appraisal has taken different forms over time but these have all shared some large-scale goals. Coens and Jenkins (2000) noted six different purposes for performance appraisal:

- Improvement
- Coaching
- Feedback
- Compensation
- Staffing decisions and professional development
- Termination/legal

Some experts praise performance reviews as an essential manage-ment tool for a variety of purposes (Battaglio, 2015). They can increase employee effectiveness and organizational success (Locke & Latham, 1990). Performance tools potentially influence the alignment of individual performance and the goals and objectives of the organization as a whole (Ayers, 2015). Well-designed performance appraisal processes provide a roadmap for interaction within the organization. This is true in educa-tion too: "Good formative assessment can generate feedback for teachers to guide their teaching and feedback for students to guide their learning" (Fullan, Hill & Crévola, 2006, p.10).

Conversely, the findings of multiple other studies indicate that performance appraisals are not fulling their intended purposes (Adler et al., 2016). In fact, a great deal of frustration is expressed in the literature over performance reviews—the extent to which they work, what to do going forward and what to do about the decades of research suggesting that the underlying foundation of the practice was wrong from the beginning (DeNisi & Smith, 2014).

Problems with Performance Appraisals in Literature

The problem with performance appraisals is not that they lack merit or do not have a positive impact in and of themselves. The issue is finding a way to incorporate them impactfully in any organization.

Employees that are supervised and evaluated are concerned about the goals, purposes, fairness and validity of the evaluation systems (Iqbal, Akbar and Budhwar, 2015). Supervisors also have their concerns with the process, the methods used, documentation, time and rating systems, and express skepticism about discussions and interactions with subordinates (Kellough & Nigro, 2002, Pooyan & Eberhardt, 1989).

The differing perceptions between supervisors and subordinates can create issues in a performance appraisal system. Inherent problems in any system include judgement errors, inflated ratings (halo effect), supervisors rating employees high who are similar to them, comparison ratings as opposed to standards, and central tendency error (Kellough, 2012, Battaglio, 2015). The literature documents performance appraisals failing for a variety of reasons (Lin & Kellough, 2019):

- The measures used to assess performance are defective (Iqbal et al., 2015).
- Lack of time, training and information regarding employee performance is a concern for supervisors (Reinke, 2003).
- Lack of authority and support.
- History of inflated ratings.

- Distribution quotas (Mohrman, Resnick-West & Lawler, 1989).
- Documentation.
- Process–product research has unsuccessfully attempted to link behaviors and traits to productivity (Kellough, 2012).
- Performance appraisals suffer from assessing what does not matter and not assessing what matters (Kellough, 2012).

Compounding all these problems is the frequent assumption that evaluations are or should be based in objective reality. In fact, subjectivity is an element of all evaluation. Heijden and Nijhof (2004) argued that

> if we look carefully at the criteria that are used in measurement scales, we will see that they don't eliminate subjectivity at all. One manager's idea of creativity can be quite different from another's idea. Any rating is only an indication of how the person (often the manager) applies a fuzzy criterion. Especially in case of a bad operationalization of the concept in question, rating systems give people a false sense of security, protection and objectivity.
>
> (Heijden & Nijhof, 2004, p. 2)

Case Study: Evaluation in Education

Jacob Easley was a high-school calculus teacher. He had attended the top state university and double majored in calculus and secondary education. He had a passion for teaching. His dad and grandfather were both teachers. His dad was a high-school chemistry teacher and his grandfather a middle-school math teacher. Jacob loved working with adolescents. He was a teacher at the high school, boys' and girls' cross-country coach and an assistant track coach. He loved his job. He was especially interested in helping students find the same level of appreciation for mathematics that he had.

After graduation Jacob was presented with several college graduate opportunities because of his knowledge and expertise in calculus. He turned down offers from several graduate school programs and private internships. He was committed to education.

During his fourth year of teaching the district hired a new superintendent. Jacob's school had always done well on the state tests. However, the other three high schools and 10 middle schools in the district were struggling to show progress on the assessments. Alongside the new superintendent the district hired a curriculum director and assistant superintendent of instruction to help "get the district back on track," academically.

At the start of his fifth year of teaching, Jacob was introduced to the new curriculum and teacher evaluation rubric. At the time, he did not think anything of it, but he would come to disagree with and dislike the new curriculum and evaluation. He did not think they aligned with his philosophy of what he knew to be true. At the district and school level there was not a lot of talk about the new systems. Jacob taught his classes and did his best. However, at the end of the year, he was dissatisfied. He thought the rubric stifled his creativity and limited his capacity to help students.

Jacob taught for two more years. As always, his students and their parents loved him, and he received good marks from his principal. However, one summer evening he came to a realization that he wanted more for his students. He wanted them to experience and learn about math with the same passion he had for the subject. He wanted the freedom to teach the students in a manner that would develop an appreciation. However, he did not think he could continue in the profession. The new evaluation system and curriculum had limited his ability to innovate, think outside the box and create learning experiences for his students. He was devastated. All he ever wanted to be was a teacher and a coach. It was part of his identity. However, that summer night he decided to accept a job from a college friend, working at a private company, analyzing environmental data to influence policy. He took the job. He was fulfilling his desire to work for something greater than himself and to do it in a free, creative atmosphere.

How often do we hear this story in education? I have seen this scenario play out at least ten times. Each time, part of the reason was the standardization of teaching through performance appraisals.

Performance of What?

If performance reviews were a drug, they would not meet FDA approval. Performance reviews in most organizations are so bad they do more harm than good.

(Sutton and Wigert, 2019)

For decades, the alarm has been sounded that the system is not working. Harry Levinson in the *Harvard Business Review* (1976) told a story of a senior executive who boosted the bottom line by several million after being told by his company president to "get it in the black." However, when the president began investigating how he bolstered the bottom line, he found that senior executive used cutthroat practices. The president learned that the executive had supplanted people who were well respected in the organization. The president told the senior advisor that unless he changed, he would likely not be promoted any further. This exposes "[t]he major fault in performance appraisal and management by objectives—namely, a fundamental misconception of what is to be appraised" (Levinson, 1976, n.p.). What the senior executive thought were being assessed were bottom-line results, while the president was more interested in the process and the way in which the senior executive achieved the results. While pleased with the results, the president understood the long-term negative impact of the methods the senior executive employed.

Those with the most experience evaluating workers are often less than positive about the opportunity. In Jena McGregor's *Washington Post* column (McGregor, 2013), Pete Juratovic, an Air Force National Guard executive, described evaluating Air Force pilots and trainees as "like a bad homework project" (n.p.).

Robert Sutton and Ben Wigert (2019), after decades of research, have told us that performance reviews may do more harm than good and that performance evaluations "communicate what is and is not important for employees to do—for better or worse" (Sutton & Wigert, 2019, n.p.). What do our teacher evaluations communicate as important?

The study of performance appraisals and performance management has become so dismal that some are even calling for the abolition of such appraisals. "Getting Rid of Performance Ratings: Genius or Folly? A Debate" (Adler et al., 2016) is an article published for the Society for Industrial and Organizational Psychology. The authors highlighted the lengthy and standing-room-only debate that ensued at the society's annual conference. They noted that performance appraisals have been an unsolved problem for multiple domains for many years.

Study after study has shown that one important component of performance management—that is, the performance review—is dreaded. Formal performance reviews are not only perceived to be of little value, they also can be highly demotivating to even the highest performing employees.

(Adler et al., 2016, p. 220)

We would be foolish to think that the education sector is immune to the problems that arise from evaluating performance. How hard is it to remove a teacher from the classroom in your state? In some states, it can take years. Are teachers improving their practice as a result of teacher evaluations? There are limited instances of documented success. Most of the research points in the other direction: teacher evaluations do not work for any of their intended purposes.

Case Study: "I Thought You Told Me to Get the Scores UP!"

We see this play out in schools often. Consider the case of Mr. Rodriguez. Mr. Rodriguez was a young, enthusiastic seventh-grade language arts teacher. He had just been employed by a middle school that had been among the highest performing in the state five years running. Mr. Rodriguez sat down with his principal, Mrs. Rhodes, at the beginning of the year. She ran him through the school's history of awards, state recognition and high scores. She explained to him that he had big shoes to fill: he was replacing a great teacher who had earned her administrative license and moved onto a principalship at a local elementary school. Mr. Rodriguez worked tirelessly his first year at the school. At the end of his first year, scores took a dip.

The school was still doing well, but his scores had slipped from the previous year and the school did not perform as well. Mr. Rodriguez was determined get the school back on top. Mrs. Rhodes was always able to offer constant reminders about the test scores.

The next year Mr. Rodriguez had the best scores in the county and the best in-school history. There was just one problem: his teaching teammates were all concerned and complaining. "Mr. Rodriguez is too hard on the kids, he demands too much, his assignments aren't meant for seventh graders, he does not follow the team's plans, he goes rogue, he's just too much." At the end of his second year, Ms. Rhodes and Mr. Rodriguez sat down to go over his annual evaluation. Any school administrator knows the rest of the story.

While Mr. Rodriguez ultimately met his and the principal's goal of increasing language arts scores, he did not go about it in the way accepted by the school community. He got the "what" but not the "how."

Mr. Rodriguez was a great teacher when he was in front of the kids. He could do it all, and teach anything. But he did it alone. He did not bring his team along with him; he alienated them and drove them away. And as a result, any gains he made with the kids came at the expense of the school culture.

It's no surprise that Ms. Rhodes was concerned, or that Mr. Rodriguez was confused. In the coming chapters we will explore the behaviors that need to be assessed in any teacher evaluation system to achieve the results Ms. Rhodes and Mr. Rodriguez were both looking for.

The Birth of the Teacher Evaluation Checklist

Evaluation in teaching, as in other fields, was born in the early twentieth century. "Objective Supervisory Tests Needed" (S.C.P., 1913), an editorial in *The Elementary School Teacher*, a University of Chicago Press journal, was one of the first documented calls for a teacher evaluation system. Some other early calls for measuring teacher competency gained attention in 1913 and 1914 with a push to attempt objective measurement of a teacher's effectiveness (Freeman, Parker, Leavilt, Bobbitt & Caldwell, 1913; Houghan, 1914). This makes one of the first documented calls for teacher evaluation tools an oxymoron—a call for one human to appraise another and eliminate the human element in the process.

In 1921, 34 school systems responded to a survey regarding the measurement of teacher effectiveness. Forty-one percent of school systems responded that they used a rating scheme for measuring teacher competency (Hill, 1921). The Duluth (MN) System for Rating Teachers (Bracken, 1922) debuted following the work of a committee of administrators and teachers. The system involved various forms and notation instructions for documenting teacher observations in the following domains: Instructional Skill, Pupil Achievement, Administrative Ability, Professional Attitude, Personal Equipment. Teachers were exclusively female and expected to follow strict protocols of behavior and dress; among the questions included were "Is her appearance favorable? Is her room neat?"

The teacher evaluation checklist would continue for another ninety years to the present day. Of course, the content of the checklists has changed over the years, but the general premise has been for principals to observe teachers teaching and to rate them according to a measurement instrument focusing mainly on the act of teaching in a classroom (Ballou, 1927; Bradley, Kallenbach, Kinney, Owen & Washington, 1964; Buck & Parsley, 1973; Peterson & Kauchak, 1982, Ford, 2018).

Beginning in the 1980s, the federal government began to initiate reform efforts in schools to ensure consistent teaching quality. It all started with the position of *A Nation at Risk* (United States National Commission on Excellence in Education, 1983). In 2001, congress passed No Child Left Behind legislation, which increased accountability for standardized testing and instituted requirements for teacher licensure.

Race to the Top (RTT) was the first attempt by the federal government to influence the evaluation or personnel component of teaching in the United States. The federal initiative motivated states to create new teacher evaluation systems that required a student data component, annual evaluations for all teachers and multiple principal observations. In the process of creating the new systems, states also created new evaluation tools or rubrics.

At least part of the reason behind the attempt to reform teacher evaluations were the beliefs that "bad" teachers were working in schools, that these teachers were not evaluated properly, that teachers' unions used poor evaluation systems to protect "bad" teachers and that principals did not have the latitude to remove the "bad" teachers. Addressing these perceived issues was the objective of the policy, which held that school leaders were not evaluating properly, or that teachers' unions had too much power over tenure issues.

Teacher Appraisal Today

Today almost every state has created teacher evaluation systems based on rubrics and principal observations in response to the requirements of the Race to the Top, requiring multiple observations of teachers and the incorporation of student learning data. Successive reform efforts have produced more of the same evaluation systems using rubrics, checklists and principal observations.

Teacher evaluation systems must be among the most contentious and counterproductive elements of the K-12 education system. Policymakers, leaders, administrators and teachers all have a dark cloud hanging over their heads as they scramble to create, implement and use a broken system.

In 2008, the American Recovery and Reinvestment Act provided $5 billion to the U.S. Department of Education to fund competitive grants for states that addressed four main policy initiatives:

- College and career-ready standards
- Developing and supporting teachers and leaders
- Data systems using technology to support instruction
- Turning around low performing schools

As a result, state legislatures and governors scrambled to create and change laws to address the four policy initiatives in order to be awarded funds through the grant. One policy that state legislatures addressed was the development of teacher and principal evaluations. Of course, the evaluations had to be linked to high-stakes assessments, and an administrator was required to conduct multiple observations throughout the school year.

In 2015, the Every Students Succeeds Act reversed the requirements imposed by the U.S. Department of Education and left teacher evaluation up to the states. However, the same assumptions about evaluating teachers effectively continue to dominate the discussion.

Researches, professionals, governments, nonprofits and foundations recognize the need for a high-quality teacher workforce. The Bill and Melinda Gates Foundation leaped into the teacher evaluation cycle with an infusion of cash. In the 2009–10 school year, the foundation committed $212 million over six years to reforming teacher evaluation systems in three large school districts: Memphis, TN, Pittsburgh, PA, Hillsborough County, FL and one California charter. With district fund-matching, the total cost of the initiative was $575 million. The Foundation established new evaluation systems, trained teachers and principals, conducted research and quickly fled when they saw no impact on student learning, growth or graduation rates. Add the almost $5 billion the federal government invested in Race to the Top, and the nation paid a steep price to do nothing in creating effective teacher evaluations.

Teacher and Principal Responses

Principals and teachers have expressed their displeasure with the system. Teachers are not confident that this process improves their practice, and view it as a compliance issue with no value (Ford, 2018).

Teachers and principals continue to express their frustration with current evaluation rubrics and observations. In a special issue of the journal *Educational Leadership* ("A Frustrating Evaluation", 2012), several teachers reported their overall frustration with the new evaluation systems. The Center on Educational Policy conducted a study representing teachers from across the United States (Renter, Kober & Frizzell, 2016). They reported similar findings. Only half of teachers reported their evaluation as helpful. Derrington & Martinez (2019) noted that teachers find the evaluation systems have a negative impact on their relationship with their principal and that they do not provide enough professional learning opportunities.

Initially, the data suggested that ineffective teachers were removed from the classroom, retired or resigned. But too often, this punished teachers who taught underprivileged children who were the hardest to teach, while failing to provide help to teachers who were struggling.

Principals are just as unfulfilled by the new systems (Flores & Derrington, 2017; Goode, 2017; Superville, 2018; Neumerski et al., 2018). Principals report that the new rubrics are too complex. They find it hard to navigate the multi-page documents and use them in a meaningful way to provide teachers with feedback. The procedures for the rubrics and systems are unclear and lack transparency. Principals consistently worry about how the evaluation systems affect school culture and relationships. Principals are also concerned about time constraints. They express the idea that the new evaluation systems take away from more important duties including community involvement and collaboration. The evidence also shows that students are not benefiting.

The book *Breakthrough* (Fullan et al., 2006) sounded the alarm that our systems and modes of operation are a barrier to the professional momentum schools need to become true learning organizations. The authors reviewed several United States policy initiatives and reflected on their failures, noting that some reforms see success from the start only to then have it fizzle out. They labeled it "A System Stalled." The reforms stalled because the change strategies implemented did not attack the root cause of the problem: "[each] new mission will require substantial changes in daily instructional practice on the part of all teachers and parallel changes in the infrastructure to support such changes" (Fullan et al., 2006, p. 4–5). When those changes don't occur, the result is failure.

The failure of school reform to improve instructional practice is fueled by mandates from outside the school, creating a lack of shared understanding, agreement and coherence in the goals, objectives, strategies and implementation of change. External accountability will yield initial results but eventually flatline.

Case Study: The Awkward Conversation

Mrs. Pung, principal at Westside High School, sat down with one of her best teachers to discuss the annual teacher performance rubric agreed upon by the school district administration and the teachers' union. She had great respect for Mr. Iott. He had been teaching industrial engineering at the high school for twenty years. Parents, students, staff—everyone loved Mr. Iott because he had so much passion. Former students had gone on to some of the top engineering schools in the country and later landed top jobs or won scholastic awards. Mrs. Pung admired Mr. Iott's passion and teaching ability. He was one of her best teachers. She thought this was going to be an easy conversation, given their positive relationship and his achievement as an educator. That is why she was so taken back by what was about to happen.

Mrs. Pung began going through the 15-page evaluation document, listing and pointing out her observations of his teaching. Mr. Iott began to pause her in disbelief: "Why am I only a 3 in lesson objectives?" Taken aback, Mrs. Pung began to fumble over her words and attempt a reasonable explanation. She thought to herself, "Did I get this wrong? Was he a 4 in this category?" She wasn't sure. She had observed Mr. Iott the required amount of times according to the collective bargaining agreement. Of course, each time she was in his room, either formally or informally, she thought nothing but the best of his teaching.

Mr. Iott had heard rumors at the last union meeting about a performance pay stipend that would be coming at the end of the year through a grant. He was worried that his overall rating would be affected by the few 3s he had received on the feedback form, even though almost all of the marks he received on the 15-page document were 4s.

Mrs. Pung started to stress out. She did not want to upset perhaps her one of her greatest assets in the science department, and perhaps the entire school. Had she missed something? Was she being unfair? If she changed his score, would she have to change other teacher's scores?

Their relationship was never the same. The endless checking of boxes, the time constraints, district-level administrative pressure, the teachers' union, and the evaluation system had them both in a box. Mr. Iott went on to take a position at another school and eventually moved into university teaching. But the questions always loomed in both of their heads: "Could it have been different? Was there a better way?"

This conversation happens in every school in the country every May. The overwhelming, troubling ramifications of this conversation will be all to easy for principals to recognize. It is a culture killer.

Since Mr. Iott has left the school, what do Mrs. Pung's superiors think about her leadership? What do fellow staff members think about the direction of the school if one of the top teachers does not even want to be there anymore? What do the parents of Mr. Iott's students think about the school and Mrs. Pung now that the man who did so much for their own kids has left?

Here we are decades removed from the Duluth administrators and teachers using checklists and ratings to evaluate teachers. Nothing has changed, and annual evaluations continue to this day in a mode of compliance with laws and policies imparted to us through the federal government, state governments and departments of education.

Where Do We Go From Here?

We are all learners. We have all had a teaching partner, a peer or a fellow administrator that we have gone to for advice, strategies, direction or feedback. But learning from others remains at the margins of what we do, not the center. However noble our efforts, we do not engage in lifelong learning as an ingrained process by which we function, move and improve in schools. At the end of the day, the prevailing thought goes "I am responsible for me, my classroom or my school. That is a special education issue, or a human resources issue."

These barriers can be hard to break down. We speak the right words about making continuing education a priority, and we may even have structures that attempt to make this possible. But our own systems, and some imposed on us by policy, get in the way. We know we have to be a team; we know we have to collaborate and work together. But when it is all said and done, we are comfortable closing our classroom door, working in isolation and being judged on our own merits—as if such a thing existed.

Any real educator knows that first graders will not be successful without a great Kindergarten experience. Any high school teacher knows that students will struggle in challenging courses without great middle school teachers to prepare them. We know we need each other, but at the end of the day we feel we are only in control of our own performance. The truth is, we are more dependent upon each other than we could ever imagine or admit. It is time to break down the massive barrier of individualistic, observation-oriented teacher evaluations and begin to cultivate our own collective efficacy.

Teaching and education are unique professional endeavors. Educators share some experiences with other professionals, but in education, children are the clients. They come to us with a variety of experiences, situations, circumstances, abilities, dispositions and cultures. The variability of our clients creates an environment that cannot be standardized. There is no agreement from research on what constitutes teaching, or even good teaching: "A consensus may not be possible or practical" (Hazi, 2018, p. 188). I believe under the current system's assumptions and given the prioritized importance of teacher behaviors exhibited in the classroom in isolation, Hazi is correct. Therefore, it is time to redefine effective teaching.

The Learning Organization

One text that leaders of all organizations should consider consulting is Peter Senge's (1990) *The Fifth Discipline: The Art & Practice of the Learning Organization*. This text is heavy reading; I found myself going back and forth rereading sections and piecing together its meaning. One thing that struck me was Senge's assertion that organizations cannot become learning organizations until schools change: "Learning organizations are possible because deep down, we are all learners" (Senge, 1990, p. 4).

While the whole text is applicable to the work we do in schools, Senge has one section devoted to education, with the subheading "Education for the 21st Century," that is particularly relevant. In this section he calls for learner-centered schools. We use this term and others such as "student-centered," "personalized learning," "student collaboration," "project-based learning" or "learning environments" to describe a way of teaching focused on each learner's needs and strengths. Senge's book highlights its importance—if people don't acquire the skills in school to become lifelong learners, other institutions will suffer.

Michael Fullan's "New Pedagogies for Deep Learning" initiative coincides with the concepts in *The Fifth Discipline*. "Deep learning" is all about changing the way our education systems operate so that children can become active learners with global competencies who understand the world as a system. The job of the school is to cultivate that curiosity, collaboration and problem solving. What better sector to lead the way as a learning organization than our schools?

Current teacher evaluation systems are dead. The individualistic, observational evaluations never worked anyway. Educational leaders should demand of policymakers that the work teachers and principals do to increase student achievement turns into the new evaluation, leveraging the power of collective efficacy and increasing student achievement.

Good formative assessments are developed by teacher teams. Good feedback for teachers comes from being a part of a learning community. To create success, leaders must put in place systematic structures to encourage those behaviors and get rid of structures that discourage those behaviors.

However, what if we could develop a system that evaluates learning organization and professional learning community principles as broad constructs to engage teachers in an unprecedented era of professionalism?

A Lasting Legacy

It has been hard for managers and administrators of any organization to operate around the concept of performance appraisals. There are no easy answers to the issues that encompass performance appraisals in education or any other sector. Even with all of their shortcomings, performance appraisals continue as mainstream practice in most organizations to this day. Performance appraisals communicate what is expected of employees on the job. Teacher evaluations, and any other evaluation, serve as the guideposts for what individual employees need to do. A problem with teacher evaluations is that the rubrics used to evaluate teachers do not communicate the most critical actions teachers can take to increase professional learning or student learning. Teacher evaluations are built on an unstable foundation of teacher isolation and research-based instructional strategies. The federal government has loosened their restrictions on teacher evaluations. States, districts and schools have an opportunity to redesign the system to incorporate learning organization principles, and finally assess what teachers do that matters most: collaboration, teamwork, collective efficacy.

Tips and Talking Points

ESSA Flexibility

By the end of the 2015–2016 school year 88% of states and the District of Columbia had recreated and instituted new teacher evaluation systems. The Every Student Succeeds Act (ESSA) has no teacher or principal evaluation requirements. In essence, states can now create their own teacher evaluation systems aligned to their own standards and constructs. The problem is that state legislators are not interested in making any more changes right now. One thing they hear from educators often is that things change too much and too quickly. I had a conversation with a state representative in my home state (Indiana). Their focus right now is funding, not evaluation. Also, state departments of education have resisted changing their modes of operation because it would mean vast amounts of internal restructuring. District leaders are also unaware of how ESSA changes could positively impact them. They are busy with the day-to-day operations of their own districts and don't have time to lobby policymakers regarding evaluations. We have also been operating in a mode of dysfunction for so long.

- *The Efficiency Ratings of Teachers* (Hill, 1921)
- *The Duluth System for Rating Teachers* (Bracken, 1922)
- *The Measurement of Teachers* (Toops, 1923)
- *How do we Know a Good Teacher?* (Biber & Snyder, 1947)
- *Measuring Teacher Competence. Research Backgrounds and Current Practice* (Bradley et al., 1964)
- *The Way We See It: A Survey of Teacher Evaluation Policies and Practices Operant in the State of Washington* (Buck & Parsley, 1973)
- *Evaluating Teacher Performance. ERS Report* (Kowalski, 1978)
- *Teacher Evaluation: Perspectives, Practices and Promises* (Peterson & Kauchak, 1982)
- *Teacher Evaluation: The Limits of Looking* (Stodolsky, 1984)
- *Choosing the Right Process for Teacher Evaluation* (Gullatt & Ballard, 1998)
- No Child Left Behind Act – 2001
- Race to the Top Act – 2009
- Every Student Succeeds Act – 2015
- *Pointing teachers in the wrong direction: Understanding Louisiana elementary teachers' use of Compass high-stakes teacher evaluation data* (Ford, 2018)

Figure 1.1 Key texts in teacher evaluation history

Evaluations have become a compliance issue and that is all. Most administrators and teachers know that the evaluation system means very little and educators have found themselves in a circle of passivity. Educators can be influenced to take the path of least resistance. However, isn't our profession more than that? Don't our kids deserve better? Isn't a teacher's professional worth greater than can be measured using a checklist?

The new teacher evaluation systems implemented in response to Race to the Top funding are no different to the old ones. "The result seems to be that across the board, states are requiring, endorsing, or recommending teacher evaluation systems that are the same or slightly different versions of the previously required systems" (Rosen & Parise, 2017, p. 12). States received the requirements from the federal government and did precisely what they should not have done: created a slight variation of the same old system. States checked a box on a federal accountability rubric and now desire principals to check boxes on teachers. Enough is enough! The system of compliance that resulted from federal legislation is killing our profession.

Now is the time to act. The federal government has loosened the restrictions on states regarding teacher evaluations. Principals need to start sounding the alarm. After all, it is the principals who have been tasked with carrying out these meaningless mandates. This is a call to action. Start having conversations. If you know a state representative, inform them of how these systems are playing out on a day-to-day basis our schools. If you can speak with district leadership, encourage them to think about creating systems of evaluation that will actually be worth something. If you have a good relationship with your teachers or a teachers' union, ask them their thoughts, begin a collaborative conversation and problem-solve the issue. Administrators will never get anywhere without the support of state legislators, district-level leadership or teachers. We can make a difference, but we must act now.

References

Adler, S., Campion, M., Colquitt, A., Grubb, A., Murphy, K., Ollander-Krane, R., & Pulakos, E. D. (2016). Getting rid of performance ratings: Genius or folly? A debate. *Industrial and Organizational Psychology*, *9*(2), 219–252.

Ayers, R. S. (2015). Aligning individual and organizational performance: Goal alignment in federal government agency performance appraisal programs. *Public Personnel Management*, 44, 169–191.

Ballou, F. W. (1927). Determining who are superior teachers. *Elementary School Journal*, *28*(4), 256.

Battaglio, R. P. (2015). Public human resource management: Strategies and practices in the 21st century. Los Angeles, CA: Sage.

Bracken, J. L. (1922). The Duluth system for rating teachers. *The Elementary School Journal*, *23*(2), 110–119.

Bradley, R., Kallenbach, W., Kinney, L., Owen, V. M., & Washington, E. (1964). *Measuring teacher competence: Research backgrounds and current practice*. Burlingame, CA: California Teachers Association.

Buck, J. J., & Parsley, J. F. (1973). *The way we see it: A survey of teacher evaluation policies and practices operant in the State of Washington*. Seattle, WA: School Information and Research Service. Retrieved from https://files.eric.ed.gov/fulltext/ED084223.pdf.

Cappelli, P., & Tavis, A. (2016, October 1). The performance management revolution. *Harvard Business Review*, October 2016.

Coens, T., & Jenkins, M. (2000). *Abolishing performance appraisals: Why they backfire and what to do instead*. San Francisco, CA: Berrett-Koehler.

DeNisi, A., & Smith, C. E. (2014). Performance appraisal, performance management, and firm-level performance: A review, a proposed model, and new directions for future research. *Academy of Management Annals, 8*(1), 127–179.

Derrington, M. L., & Martinez, J. A. (2019). Exploring teachers' evaluation perceptions: A snapshot. *NASSP Bulletin, 103*(1), 32–50.

Flores, M. A., & Derrington, M. L. (2017). School principals' views of teacher evaluation policy: Lessons learned from two empirical studies. *International Journal of Leadership in Education, 20*(4), 416–431.

Ford, T. G. (2018). Pointing teachers in the wrong direction: Understanding Louisiana elementary teachers' use of Compass high-stakes teacher evaluation data. *Educational Assessment, Evaluation and Accountability, 30*(3), 251–283.

Freeman, F. N., Parker, S. C., Leavilt, F. M., Bobbitt, J. F., & Caldwell, O. W. (1913). Educational news and editorial comment. *The Elementary School Teacher, 14*(4), 145–157.

A Frustrating Evaluation Experience. (2012). *Educational leadership, 70*(3), 90–91.

Fullan, M., Hill, P., & Crévola, C. (2006). *Breakthrough*. Thousand Oaks, CA: Corwin Press.

Goode, H. (2017). Why is job frustration on the rise among school principals? Global Teletherapy. Retrieved from https://globalteletherapy.com/job-frustration/.

Hazi, H. M. (2018). Coming to understand the wicked problem of teacher evaluation. In S. J. Zepeda & J. A. Ponticell (Eds.), *The Wiley handbook of educational supervision* (pp. 183–207). Hoboken, NJ: John Wiley & Sons, Inc.

Heijden, B. I. J. M. van der, & Nijhof, A. H. J. (2004). The value of sub-jectivity: Problems and prospects for 360-degree appraisal systems. *The International Journal of Human Resource Management, 15*(3), 493–511.

Hill, C. W. (1921). The efficiency ratings of teachers. *The Elementary School Journal, 21*(6), 438–443.

Houghan, F. R. (1914). Efficiency of teachers. *The Journal of Education, 79*(5 (1965)), 120.

Iqbal, M. Z., Akbar, S., & Budhwar, P. (2015). Effectiveness of perform-ance appraisal: An integrated framework. *International Journal of Management Reviews, 17*, 510–533.

Kellough, J. E. (2012). Managing human resources to improve organizational productivity: The role of performance evaluation. In N. M. Riccucci (Ed.), *Public personnel management: Current, concerns, future challenges* (pp. 173–185). Boston, MA: Longman.

Kellough, J. E., & Nigro, L. G. (2002). Pay for performance in Georgia state government: Employee perspectives of Georgia Gain after 5 years. *Review of Public Personnel Administration, 22,* 146–166.

Levinson, H. (1976). Appraisal of what performance? *Harvard Business Review, July 1976.*

Lin, Y.-C., & Kellough, J. E. (2019). Performance appraisal problems in the public sector: Examining supervisors' perceptions. *Public Personnel Management, 48*(2), 179–202. https://doi.org/10.1177/0091026018801045.

Locke, E. A., & Latham, G. P. (1990). A theory of goal setting and task performance. Upper Saddle River, NJ: Prentice Hall.

McGregor, J. (2013, February 14). *The corporate kabuki of performance review. The Washington Post.* Retrieved from www.washingtonpost.com/.

Mohrman, A. M., Resnick-West, S. M., & Lawler, E. E. (1989). Designing performance appraisal systems: Aligning appraisals and organizational realities. San Francisco, CA: Jossey-Bass.

Murphy, K. R., Cleveland, J. N., & Hanscom, M. E. (2018). *Performance appraisal and management.* Los Angeles, CA: SAGE Publications.

Neumerski, C. M., Grissom, J. A., Goldring, E., Drake, T. A., Rubin, M., Cannata, M., & Schuermann, P. (2018). Restructuring instructional leadership: How multiple-measure teacher evaluation systems are redefining the role of the school principal. *The Elementary School Journal, 119*(2), 270–297.

Peterson, K., & Kauchak, D. (1982). *Teacher evaluation: Perspectives, practices, and promises.* Salt Lake City, UT: University of Utah Center for Educational Practice.

Pooyan, A., & Eberhardt, B. J. (1989). Correlates of performance appraisal satisfaction among supervisory and nonsupervisory employees. *Journal of Business Research, 19,* 215–226.

Reinke, S. J. (2003). Does the form really matter? Leadership, trust, and acceptance of the performance appraisal process. *Review of Public Personnel Administration, 23*(1), 23–37.

Renter, D. S., Kober, N., & Frizzell, M. (2016) *Listen to us: Teacher views and voices*. Washington, DC: Center on Education Policy. Retrieved from www.cep-dc.org/displayDocument.cfm?DocumentID=1456.

Rosen, R., & Parise, L. M. (2017). Using evaluation systems for teacher improvement: Are school districts ready to meet new federal goals? New York and Oakland, CA: MDRC. Retrieved from www.semanticscholar.org/paper/Using-Evaluation-Systems-for-Teacher-Improvement%3A-Rosen-Parise/bda6a3b29c912a659abe07f34f444e3059d56ce7

S. C. P. (1913). Objective supervisory tests needed. *Elementary School Teacher, 14*(4), 149.

Senge, P. M. (1990). *The fifth discipline: the art and practice of the learning organization*. New York: Doubleday/Currency.

Superville, D. R. (2018). Teacher Evaluations Stretch Principals' Expertise, Time. *Education Week; Bethesda, 38*(13), 6.

Sutton, R., & Wigert, B. (2019). More harm than good: The truth about performance reviews. Retrieved from www.gallup.com/workplace/249332/harm-good-truth-performance-reviews.aspx.

United States National Commission on Excellence in Education. (1983). A nation at risk: the imperative for educational reform. Washington, DC: National Commission on Excellence in Education.

Current Teacher Evaluations Systems Overview

How Are Teachers Being Evaluated?

Explore the Department of Education website of any state and you will find documents ranging in length from fifty to one hundred (or even hundreds of) pages explaining their state's teacher evaluation system. It is sometimes hard to even understand what the objective is, or how to get there, by reading through these documents. Dozens of teacher practices to evaluate, along with so-called Value-Added Measures (VAMs) and student growth calculations, render the process mind-bogglingly confusing.

The Colorado Department of Education (CDE) has a host of documents to review for their teacher evaluation system. Clicking through the CDE website (www.cde.state.co.us/educatoreffectiveness/smes-teacher) reveals a trove of documents, rubrics and guides to begin learning about the system. Colorado has changed its system three times since its initial Race to the Top application, in 2011, 2013 and 2017. Teachers are categorized as "Basic," "Partially Proficient," "Proficient," "Accomplished" or "Exemplary." The rubrics have been scaled back as they have been revised. The documents started with 5 standards, 27 elements and 309 professional practices. The latest rubric has 4 standards, 17 elements and 165 professional practices.

Let's try some simple math. Take an average-size elementary school with 20 certified teachers. Multiplying 20 by 165 gives 3,300—that is 3,300 professional judgements a principal will have to make each year for an entire staff. And that's without addressing their inter-rater agreement systems and document—a 12-page document with fancy bubbles, maps, arrows and explanations, each addressing what to do in the inevitable event that two people observing the same teacher assign them different numbers.

Each state is different and has gone down its own rabbit hole of impracticality. Florida has basic standards; local districts create their own systems which must be approved by the State. A simple look into the Broward County public schools teacher evaluation system yields a 154-page policy manual (School District of Broward County, 2019), with various charts, rubrics, "crosswalks" and annual cycles, informal and formal, including "walkthroughs." (Teacher evaluation seems to breed new terms whose meaning is unclear.) Classroom teachers can be labeled "Exemplary," "Accomplished," "Proficient," "Emergent" and "Needed," with a final rating for "High Effective," "Effective," "Needs Improvement" and "Unsatisfactory." Different categories and domains yield varying weighted percentages for deliberate practice, "legacy models," classroom models and non-classroom models. And if you were hired on or before a certain date, or on or after the 99th day of school, you are placed into varying cyclical evaluation timetables.

A teacher can also be classed as one of three different effectiveness levels—"lower," "middle" and "upper"—based on a decimal point scale. The Broward County, Florida teacher evaluation manual aims to clarify the system with a graphic that, as the caption states, "Illustrate[s] how a fourth-grade teacher and a ninth-grade English language arts teacher can earn a highly effective and an unsatisfactory summative performance rating, respectively" (School District of Broward County, 2019, p. 14).

The last rubric highlighted in the Broward County manual is the Marzano rubric. It appears in the manual without an explanation as to why it is there. Go to any state website and you will find a similar system with rubrics, charts, graphs, percentages, decimal points, categories, scoring forms, ratings forms, calculation FAQs and a litany of terms, lists, bullet points and checkboxes.

The Nevada Department of Education (2020) has a similar system. Appendix D on page 33 of their evaluation manual attempts to explain and define the various levels and indicators using complex explanations:

LEVEL 4 All Students: To receive a Performance Level 4, a teacher needs to demonstrate that all the students are being well served by instruction. This is indeed a high bar which teachers may strive for, yet not fully reach. If the evaluator, through direct observation, is able to judge that all but one or two students are being addressed with respect to the indicator, then the teacher must demonstrate through other evidence sources that he or she has made every possible effort to reach the all student status.

(Nevada Department of Education, 2020, p. 43)

A teacher in Nevada has to go to great lengths to prove their effectiveness.

These policies claim to be well intentioned. For example, Michigan claims that "Implementing Michigan's educator evaluation law with fidelity is a key strategy in our efforts to see Michigan become a top ten education state within the next ten years" (Michigan Department of Education, 2019, p. 4), But these systems reveal a lack of knowledge about their actual impact or the practice of teaching. These states are not alone. Just about every state in the country has a similar system, making the same faulty assumptions regarding the evaluation of teaching quality.

The Marzano Teacher Evaluation Model

The Marzano Teacher Evaluation Model, as adopted by the state of Washington amongst other states (Marzano & Tooth, 2013), has four main domains. Each domain has numbered elements with anywhere from three to eight points to check off for "Teacher Evidence" and "Student Evidence." In all, there are 58 elements within the four domains. Within those 58 elements, there are 336 points of evidence.

The Danielson Framework

The Framework for Teaching (2013), originally created by Danielson (2007) and used in hundreds of school districts around the country, describes a framework for effective teaching. The framework consists of four domains: "Planning and Preparation," "The Classroom Environment," "Instruction" and "Professional Responsibilities." In total, *The Framework for Teaching* has 86 points of emphasis, classifying teachers as "unsatisfactory," "basic," "proficient" or "distinguished," with several bullet points under each category.

Indiana RISE Teacher Evaluation Model

This model, developed in 2011, is in use throughout the state of Indiana. The Indiana RISE Evaluation and Development System (Indiana Department of Education, n.d.) can be viewed on the Indiana Department of Education's website. The rubric prints off on 11x14 inch paper, is 15 pages long and has 259 points of emphasis. There are four main domains, three of which are broken down into "Highly Effective," "Effective," "Improvement Necessary" and "Ineffective" categories. The first domain, "Planning," is worth 10% of the final score. The second domain encompasses aspects of teaching and learning during a classroom lesson. This accounts for 75% of the final score. The third domain, "Leadership," is worth 15% of the final score. The fourth domain encompasses "core professionalism," consisting of attendance, on-time arrival, policies and procedures and respect. Domain 4 is assessed as satisfactory or unsatisfactory. Indiana has removed the requirement for student achievement and growth data to be included in a teacher's final rating as a percentage, along with the score teachers receive on the observation evaluation rubric.

Current Systems Don't Work

These long evaluations aren't just painful to fill out; they are ineffective at increasing student learning and achievement. Recognition of the problems with current evaluation methods is growing (Gabriel, 2017; Hoge, 2016; Danielson, 2016). A recent *Education Week* blog post noted that the Bill and Melinda Gates Foundation has pulled its resources and funds from helping reshape the teacher evaluation systems in this country (Iasevoli, 2018). The RAND Corporation released the results of their study regarding teacher performance evaluations and student achievement under the Bill and Melinda Gates Foundation's Measure of Effectiveness (MET) project. The results showed that, after three years of implementing new teacher evaluation rubrics, there was no correlation between teacher performance on the rubrics and student achievement (Stecher et al., 2018). Foundation decision-makers are starting to realize that there are fundamental flaws with evaluation systems throughout the nation, and that these evaluations have no impact on student learning and achievement. Medlock (2017) and

Alexander, Jang & Kankane (2017) have pointed out that current teacher performance evaluations have no effect on closing the achievement gap for Black or Latino students.

Michael Schmoker, in his *Education Week* article "Why Complex Teacher Evaluations Don't Work" (2012), pointed out that "these jargon-laced, confusing documents are to be used to evaluate or even to compensate teachers on the basis of multiple, full-period, pre-announced classroom observations" (n.p.). Schmoker continued, "like so many past reforms, this one will be launched nationally, like a bad movie, without being piloted and refined first. (Imagine if we did this with prescription drugs)" (n.p.). Schmoker's criticism is accurate. Teacher evaluation documents are confusing and offer no real solutions. Because they are heavily standardized, they encompass what we know as effective strategies, but do not take into account the needs of the local teachers, students or schools, or the needs of the organization as a whole.

Federal involvement in teacher evaluation policy resulted in a few things. First, the creation of comprehensive evaluation tools and rubrics. Second, the use of student data. Third, multiple classroom observations of teachers and an annual evaluation for every teacher. Classroom observation of teachers using a rubric of effective teaching was a component of each state's new evaluation system in response to RTT (Hallgren et al., 2014). The basic line of thinking is that student achievement data and principals observing teachers, providing feedback, will help identify bad teachers and help the effective teachers become even better. Together with student achievement and growth data, observation data and feedback should give the teacher enough information to improve and justify their effectiveness.

Teachers Are Still Dissatisfied

Educators have long agreed with researchers about the weaknesses of evaluation methods. Robert Wolf (1973) reported the following:

> Teachers...believe that the standards for evaluating...are too vague and ambiguous to be worth anything. They feel that current appraisal techniques fall short of collecting information that accurately characterizes their performance. They perceive the ultimate rating as depending more on the idiosyncrasies of the rater rather than on their own behavior in the classroom. As a

result, teachers see nothing to be gained from evaluation. ...present teacher evaluation practice does more to interfere with professional quality teaching than to nurture it.

(Wolf, 1973, p. 160)

It seems as though little has changed since Robert Wolf was conducting his research on teacher evaluations in the 1970s.

In an article in the *Miami Herald* (Gurney, 2016, n.p.) one teacher expressed his frustration, ""They're killing us this year with morale," said Shawn Beightol, a chemistry teacher at John A. Ferguson Senior High School. "It's like the straw that broke the camel's back. There are teachers quitting right now because of this." Teachers are quitting and high-school and college students are not even considering the profession because of teacher evaluations.

Kraft et al. (2018) laid out the scenario pretty plainly: people are choosing to avoid the education profession because of high-stakes evaluations. Charlotte Danielson, the creator of one widely used evaluation system, has herself expressed concern that nurturing great teaching has become a difficult task to complete in policy and practice (Danielson, 2016). Danielson elaborated, "I'm deeply troubled by the transformation of teaching from a complex profession requiring nuanced judgement to the performance of certain behaviors that can be ticked off on a checklist" (Danielson, 2016, n.p.). Danielson argued that future evaluation systems should encourage professional learning, inquiry and trust.

Why are these systems so ineffective? I argue current systems don't work because they all rest on false assumptions. The maturation of teaching quality rubrics defining the work will never be able to match the complexity and nuance of teaching. Creating and using complex documents actually hinders the maturation of effective teaching.

Complexity of the Work is Good, Complexity in Documents is Cumbersome

Current evaluation systems do include some items that reflect quality teaching. But they're too complex. They are hard for teachers and administrators to implement and do not place enough emphasis on the few things teachers do that matter most: collaboration, taking part in professional learning communities, building student, family and collegial relationships and creating engaging, research-based lessons.

One of the main publicized intentions of the evaluation systems approved through Race to the Top is the firing of bad teachers (Lavigne, 2014). The assumptions that give this intention validity are grounded in deficit thinking—the belief that failure is cause by an individual's inherent deficiencies or traits they lack. Our evaluations focus on the least effective and have little to offer those who are performing well. Berliner (2018) estimated that 3–6% of the nation's teachers are ineffective. We implemented an evaluation system to address a small percentage of teachers. We are also finding that ineffective teachers are not being removed from the classroom. Current systems of teacher evaluation are not able to identify or remove bad teachers.

This "deficit" model is opposed to a system that focuses on the effective teachers and their ability to influence student achievement. We need tools that focus our attention on making the good teachers we have better. Instead of measuring effectiveness, we need to evaluate teacher effectiveness and let the local schools and teachers drive the improvement.

The theory in performance appraisals is that by improving individual performance we can improve the performance of the organization. There is very limited research to suggest that this is possible (DeNisi & Smith, 2014). Standardized knowledge, skills and abilities must be translated into specific terms to improve organization-level performance (DeNisi & Smith, 2014).

Why are we evaluating teachers based on their ability to deliver lessons, when it is the work that happens *before* the lessons that has the largest effect on student achievement? Current teacher evaluation systems stifle instructional leadership because they evaluate a teacher's performance in isolation.

Case Study: The Teacher Evaluation Process

Mrs. Jones was a veteran teacher with 23 years' experience. She was highly regarded by students, parents, teachers and her past four principals. Her third graders always grew. Of course, achievement scores were usually very good, with their normal ups and downs. But Mrs. Jones knew her students. She could sit down with a parent and in 15 minutes paint a complete reader profile of the student, and send the parent home with a few things to work on to continue to stimulate their reading development. That is one thing Mrs. Jones always understood: that learning to read is a developmental process. She knew how to develop good, healthy readers.

Mrs. Jones sat down with her principal at the beginning of the year, as they had in years past, to go over the evaluation rubric, evaluation processes and timelines and set goals for student achievement. Mrs. Jones and Mrs. Smith both expressed their mutual appreciation for one another and what they each did to serve students and families. Mrs. Jones and Mrs. Smith both signed the required paperwork and went on their way.

A few weeks later Mrs. Smith was making her way into classrooms to conduct her formal observations of teachers for their evaluations. She stopped by Mrs. Jones' room. Mrs. Smith would not have described the classroom as a disaster, but the kids did seem a little off and Mrs. Jones was clearly not at her best. Mrs. Smith did see the bulk of reading instruction and knew things were not progressing as Mrs. Jones had wished. Mrs. Smith also saw Mrs. Jones bring the kids back together and make a few links in the literary elements before the kids went to recess. Mrs. Smith thought Mrs. Jones did a great job bringing the kids back together and refocusing them before a break. Mrs. Smith conducted her evaluation and forgot about it. She knew Mrs. Jones was great. One observation was not going to flip her opinion of Mrs. Jones' abilities. However, the scenario stuck with Mrs. Jones for weeks. She was devastated that her principal saw her and her students on a bad day.

Mrs. Jones and Mrs. Smith sat down at the end of the year to go over student data, observation notes and rubric scores to determine Mrs. Jones placement on the effectiveness continuum. Mrs. Jones was a nervous wreck. She was sure that her evaluation would be reflective of her scores during one of Mrs. Smith's observations. To her surprise she was rated exactly the same as last year, "Highly Effective." Mrs. Smith again told Mrs. Jones how much she appreciated her. They had a conversation about the tremendous growth that all of her students had made this year, just as in years past. Mrs. Jones asked Mrs. Smith about the poor observation and if that came into account. Mrs. Smith reiterated her previous thoughts to Mrs. Jones: "One observation is not going to taint what I already know about your teaching ability." Mrs. Jones was relieved.

In this scenario, Mrs. Jones is lucky she has a good working relationship with Mrs. Smith and that they know each other professionally very well. Some people would say that Mrs. Smith acted unprofessionally or even unethically, or at the very least that she was not following the system.

The problem isn't with Mrs. Smith's actions—it's with what she was being asked to do. Imagine a college football coach observing each one of his starting offensive and defensive players perform their set of skills and drills individually for 30–45 minutes at a time, spending another 30 minutes writing a narrative about what he saw, and then having a 30-minute meeting with the athlete about what was observed. When would the coaching staff create the vision for the team, set the direction of the offensive and defensive schemas, watch film, scout other teams, analyze data and recruit new players? Where is the time for press conferences, community relations and NCAA compliance? Coaches do not evaluate players in this manner. They observe, collaborate, assess, complete needs-based assessments, provide learning opportunities through instruction and conduct position meetings, skill clinics and film sessions with multiple coaches and teammates at the same time. Schools, educators, teachers and principals can implement the type of learning communities that benefit college football teams.

All teacher evaluation documents incorporate some sound strategies, behaviors and techniques. The problem is the context in which they are used and their ability to influence the increase in collective efficacy needed to improve. The evaluation documents highlighted in this chapter, and many more just like them, are great documents to be used by collaborative teams to decide how they are going to teach lessons, solve problems, meet student needs and implement tailored pedagogical practices. They should not be used to assess overall effectiveness.

Teacher Evaluation Ratings

Kraft and Gilmour (2017) examined the distribution of ratings teachers have received across several states, and reported that "the percentage of teachers rated as Unsatisfactory has not changed in the majority of states that have adopted new teacher evaluation systems" (p. 4). In other words, the teacher evaluation reforms neither increased or decreased the number of teachers rated as satisfactory or unsatisfactory. The authors ask, "Does the distribution of teacher performance ratings reflect evaluators' perceptions about the distribution of teacher effectiveness? And, if not, what are evaluators' explanations for why teacher evaluation reforms have not resulted in greater differentiation in performance ratings?" (p. 4) I think the overwhelming body of research on performance appraisals can answer those questions. Education is not immune to organization psychology issues or questions.

I believe this happens for understandable reasons. Subjective performance evaluations pose challenges for assessing effectiveness, mainly in the form of bias from the evaluator (Bol & Smith, 2011). One form this bias takes is the halo effect (Jacobs & Kozlowski, 1985), in which evaluators rate a person's performance as high because their overall opinion of that person is positive. The halo effect introduces biases from the rater into the evaluation system (Bol & Smith, 2011). In the case of teacher evaluation, principals perceive teachers as having little control over test scores and therefore inflate their observational ratings subconsciously. Geiger and Amrein-Beardsley (2017) have implied that principals are "gaming" the teacher evaluation systems. By contrast, I believe there is ample research regarding the halo effect as a reasonable explanation for lack of distribution in teacher effectiveness ratings.

A more practical reason for lack of distribution of teacher effectiveness ratings is that the current system is impractical and disconnected from the real work that teachers and principals do. Principal observations of teachers have become a matter of compliance only. Principals complete teacher observations because they are mandated, not because completing them is the most effective way to improve adult and student learning or performance. Observing a 30- to 45-minute lesson by an individual teacher is low on the list of priorities for school leaders. Higher on the list is collaboration, setting goals, analyzing data and assisting teachers in lesson planning, curriculum mapping and professional learning. Principals are also responsible for student management, community engagement and outreach and parent relations. Principals give all teachers similar ratings because effectively evaluating teachers with a confusing and often wordy rubric is impractical. Using a document that has multiple pages (sometimes 15–45 pages) encompassing effective teaching components, during a classroom observation, is not how schools, teachers, principals or students improve. Teachers do not grow professionally by being "assessed." Teachers grow professionally by being active members in a professional learning community, which in return has a positive impact on student achievement (Saunders, Goldenberg & Gallimore, 2009).

Teacher evaluations do not reflect the evaluators' perception of individual teachers' actual strengths and weaknesses because the rubrics are too long and complex, are not personalized or differentiated and take too much time to conduct, write up and discuss. Principals do not have enough time to evaluate teachers through a mostly observational model (DuFour & Mattos, 2013). Kraft and Gilmour reported similar findings in their 2017 study.

It's Not the People—It's the System

> The more any quantitative social indicator is used for social decision-making, the more subject it will be to corruption pressures and the more apt it will be to distort and corrupt the social processes it is intended to monitor.
>
> (Campbell, 1976, p. 49)

The problem isn't that principals are doing a bad job of observing and rating teachers. It's that they're being asked to do something (rate performance objectively and consistently) that's been proven to be impossible.
Inter-rater reliability—or the degree to which multiple people observing something will rate or categorize it in the same way—has been a challenging topic in many domains for over one hundred years. Scholars, organizational psychologists and business leaders still do not have all the answers. It is presumptuous to think that teachers or education policymakers will. The California teacher evaluation system was the subject of a 2010 study by Porter; the results showed no consistency between raters. This isn't unique to teaching. We will discuss inter-rater reliability later in Tips and Talking Points.

Measurement vs. Evaluation

The problems with reliability are compounded when those doing evaluations believe or are told that they're measuring something objectively.
The late education researcher Thomas Sergiovanni addressed teacher evaluation and its flaws alongside his colleague Robert Starratt. Their 2007 book *Supervision: A Redefinition* gave a background to the issue and

defined terms for educators. Measurement in teacher supervision refers to the act of observing the teaching and assessing it against a tool, rubric or protocol. Evaluation is the act of "using discernment and making informed judgements" (Sergiovanni & Starratt, 2007, p. 174). Supervision is a very human process that requires a certain level of trust, respect and relationship. Measurement tools apply to all teachers in all situations. An evaluation would consist of the teacher making decisions about what to do and how to do it in the context of their school, classroom and student needs.

We have made the terms "measurement" and "evaluation" synonymous, when in fact they are distinctly different. The authors discuss criterion-referenced evaluations, which are very similar to measurement systems. In criterion-referenced systems the evaluator is looking for purposes and values. In a measurement system an evaluator is looking for specific strategies and behaviors.

Most of the states in the United States use a system that is a mixture of teacher measurement and a criterion-referenced system: "By and large neither teachers, nor administrators are very satisfied with present procedures" (Sergiovanni and Starratt, 2007, p. 169). The result, as the authors stated, is that "Too often the system takes on a certain artificial or mechanical quality, a routine functioning that becomes an end in itself" (Sergiovanni and Starratt, 2007, p.169). The process then becomes a "dog and pony show" for the teacher and a compliance requirement for the principal. The appraisal process has become too concerned with how to measure effectiveness and to little concerned to cultivate improvement of performance (DeNisi & Smith, 2014).

Patterned Rationality and the Art of Teaching

Data-driven rubrics divide teaching up into discrete tasks and categories, such as the Danielson and Marzano models summarized earlier. But this overly neat view of teaching objectives is the antithesis of how effective teaching works.

Sergiovanni and Starratt (2007) noted a phenomenon called "patterned rationality." Teachers do not think of their practice as working in a realm of goals and objectives but value patterns. Reading teachers want students

Teacher Evaluation Theory

Measurement	Evaluation
Standard Criteria	Fluid Criteria
Fixed	Adaptable
Definite	Open-Ended
Attempts Objectivity	Admittedly Subjective
Assessed Against a Tool	Tools Used to Inform Judgements and Decisions
All Situations, All the Time	Considers Context

Figure 2.1 Teacher evaluation theory

to learn the letters and their sounds and sentence structure (reading fundamentals), while at the same time they want them to be able to synthesize information and make meaning of the text. The act of teaching reading requires a healthy balance of the two.

Sometimes these objectives are in competition with one another based on the developmental needs of the student; one objective may even be more emphasized one day and not the next in order to help the student grow academically. This is particularly true in early grades, when student academic growth patterns can fluctuate very quickly. It becomes very difficult for the teacher to think about reading growth in narrow terms. Good teachers find rational patterns and move about their days with the students like a masterful artist. In literature this is referred to as patterned rationality.

Since teachers are concerned with outcomes that produce a sensible pattern (common sense for a teacher), it is difficult to ask them to think specifically in terms of this outcome or that, or even several outcomes discretely. I think the same is true for the high-school algebra teacher. By creating narrow, standardized teacher evaluation documents we are hindering the teacher's ability to influence student learning and growth, because they view the education of the student in a holistic sense, as a process of making connections and growing along the way.

As Sergiovanni and Starratt explained, teaching is a profession in which teachers find rationalistic patterns. The teacher evaluation documents in use do not reflect the realities of the practice. The documents are rational and based on "research," but—given a different context or goal and considered outside of rationalistic patterns—they become a source of immense frustration and hindrance to teachers and principals. They reduce teaching to a set of predictable modes and methods in an unpredictable environment that requires sound judgement, nuance and adaptability.

These standardized documents provide checklists calling for uniform usage that may not be appropriate for the given lesson, unit, student or circumstance. The documents assume that teaching needs to be monitored and assessed to ensure that the instruction received by the students is reliable and predictable. In fact, teaching is an art that requires the practitioner to adapt, implement and change based on what is happening and has happened in the classroom.

Collecting Data Is Not the Answer

Those who create evaluation have fallen into the rationality trap and advocated for a system of measurement of teaching (Sergiovanni & Starratt, 2007), with its charts, data, tools, rubrics, multiple observers, double scoring and other complex methods. But good evaluation is a humanistic process, not a mechanical one. We need collaborative documents that encourage teamwork, sound management principles and shared governance.

Measurement systems have a place in teaching; however, their uses are situational in a given specific context. For example, a particular chemistry experiment can be measured to assess procedures and scaffolding, implementing a lesson structure or a scripted teacher/student exchange, but not to yield a summative performance rating. What we need is an evaluation system that engages teachers' intellect, desire to collaborate and natural motivation to be successful for their students. Such a system could provide the engaging professional experience that the new generation of workers desires.

The Kane et al. (2014) book *Designing Teacher Evaluation Systems: New Guidance from the Measures of Effective Teaching Project* is a work focusing on the question "What is effective teaching?" This book is a measurement system for assessing teacher effectiveness shown to be ineffective by the RAND report. The researchers collected troves of data to find no real conclusions for evaluating teachers in a measurement system.

Models exist for the type of system we need. These include the Johns Hopkins Professional Nursing Model, which is a learning structure to help nurses make decisions, collaborate, receive feedback and have influence over patient care. Another useful model is that of professional learning communities (PLC) in education. There are a vast number of PLC tools to help teachers guide themselves to be more effective in PLC processes. These tools are just not being used in our evaluation systems in any meaningful way.

 ## Conclusion

Consult your state's or district's teacher evaluation tool. Read it with a critical eye. What behaviors does it assume or dictate? Most likely, you will be drawn to the conclusion that it assumes teachers—or the principal through "instructional leadership"—are the primary people behind the performance of the teacher. Teacher performance is cast as individualistic, taking place in a vacuum or in isolation. Teachers are singlehandedly responsible for their performance through a set of narrowly defined skills and behaviors in the classroom with their students and no one else. If the teacher would simply check for understanding at the right time, or develop the right classroom management procedures, everything would be fine… or so these tools imply.

Teacher evaluation reform is a failed policy initiative. In the next chapter, we'll turn to the foundation of the whole structure and show how faulty assumptions about how to assess teacher effectiveness have been detrimental to the profession.

Tips and Talking Points

Workforce Demands

Welcome to the Experience Economy (Pine and Gilmore, 1998) described the changes in our modern economy from commodities and goods to services and later, at a premium, experiences. Education is currently in a labor war. People do not want to enter the education field. One reason that has emerged in research is the high-stakes teacher evaluations. Think of potential teachers as the customer. Students graduating high school and college today simply don't want "a job" or even a career: they want a fulfilling professional experience. What is your experience with teacher evaluation systems? If a professional experience is what you are looking for, teaching is the last thing you want to do for a living. Experiences are memorable and create an emotional connection for those who are engaged. Think about your career: when or what were your most fulfilling moments? They probably involved experiencing the collaborative work that went into solving a problem, establishing a program or securing an accomplishment for your school or class. We can create these experiences in our current system, although it is harder to do so when your pay is tied to a lousy framework, or your perceived professional worth is wrapped up in endless rubrics, calculations and rating scales. This is a barrier we have to remove. If we don't, we won't have any teachers to teach the kids. Schools need systematic methods or operating procedures that create and reinforce a learning culture for the adults. New ways of evaluating can help aid in this endeavor.

Kraft et al. (2018) have reported that young people are not entering the teacher workforce, at least in part because of high-stakes teacher evaluations. Performance-based pay has been shown not to motivate people to enter the teaching field. High school students' interest in the teaching profession is down 3% and enrollment in teacher programs is down significantly, about 35% (Aragon, 2016). By 2025 policy researchers are estimating that the nation will be about 100,000 teachers short of the total needed to fully staff our schools, and this is going to have a disproportionate effect in high-poverty schools (García & Weiss, 2019). Has it gotten so bad that we are now advocating for robots as teachers (Edwards & Cheok, 2018)?

References

Alexander, N., Jang, S. T., & Kankane, S. (2017). The performance cycle: The association between student achievement and state policies tying together teacher performance, student achievement, and accountability. *American Journal of Education, 123*(3), 413–446.

Aoki, T., Kudo, M., Endo, M., Nakayama, Y., Amano, A., Naito, M., & Ota, Y. (2019). Inter-rater reliability of the Oral Assessment Guide for oral cancer patients between nurses and dental hygienists: The difficulties in objectively assessing oral health. *Supportive Care in Cancer, 27*(5), 1673–1677.

Aragon, S. (2016). Education commission of the states teacher shortages: What we know. Retrieved from www.ecs.org/wp-content/uploads/Teacher-Shortages-What-We-Know.pdf.

Berliner, D. C. (2018). Between Scylla and Charybdis: Reflections on and problems associated with the evaluation of teachers in an era of metrification. *Education Policy Analysis Archives, 26*, 54.

Bol, J. C., & Smith, S. D. (2011). Spillover effects in subjective performance evaluation: Bias and the asymmetric influence of controllability. *Accounting Review, 86*(4), 1213–1230.

School District of Broward County (2019). Instructional personnel evaluation system. Fort Lauderdale, FL: Broward County Public Schools. Retrieved from www.browardschools.com/Page/41770.

Campbell, D. T. (1976). Assessing the impact of planned social change. *Public Affairs Centre* Occasional Paper Series, 8. Hanover, NH: Public Affairs Center, Dartmouth College.

Danielson, C. (2007). *Enhancing professional practice: A framework for teaching* (2nd ed.). Alexandria, VA: Association for Supervision & Curriculum Development.

Danielson, C. (2016, April 20). Charlotte Danielson on rethinking teacher evaluation. *Education Week.* Retrieved from www.edweek.org/ew/articles/2016/04/20/charlotte-danielson-on-rethinking-teacher-evaluation.html.

DeNisi, A., & Smith, C. E. (2014). Performance appraisal, performance management, and firm-level performance: A review, a proposed model, and new directions for future research. *Academy of Management Annals, 8*(1), 127–179.

DuFour, R., & Mattos, M. (2013). How do principals really improve schools? *Educational Leadership, 70*(7), 34–40.

Edwards, B. I., & Cheok, A. D. (2018). Why not robot teachers: Artificial intelligence for addressing teacher shortage. *Applied Artificial Intelligence, 32*(4), 345–360.

Danielson Group (n.d.) The Framework for Teaching. Retrieved from https://danielsongroup.org/framework/framework-teaching.

Gabriel, R. (2017) Rubrics and reflection: A discursive analysis of observation debrief conversations between novice Teach for America teachers and mentors. *Action in Teacher Education. 39* (1), n.p.

García, E., & Weiss, E. (2019). *The teacher shortage is real, large and growing, and worse than we thought.* Education Policy Institute. Retrieved from https://scholar.harvard.edu/files/mkraft/files/kraft_et_al._2018_teacher_accountability_reforms.pdf

Geiger, T. J., & Amrein-Beardsley, A. (2017). Administrators gaming test- and observation-based teacher evaluation methods: To conform to or confront the system. *AASA Journal of Scholarship & Practice, 14*(3), 45–53.

Gurney, K. (2016, December 12). Teachers say it's getting harder to get a good evaluation. The school district disagrees. Miami Herald. Retrieved from www.miamiherald.com/news/local/education/article119791683.html.

Hallinger, P., Heck, R. H., & Murphy, J. (2014). Teacher evaluation and school improvement: An analysis of the evidence. *Educational Assessment, Evaluation and Accountability; Dordrecht, 26*(1), 5–28.

Hoge, D. M. (2016). The relationship between teachers' instructional practices, professional development, and student achievement. (Doctoral dissertation, University of Nebraska at Omaha).

Indiana Department of Education (n.d.). Indiana RISE rubric. Retrieved from www.doe.in.gov/sites/default/files/evaluations/rise-handbook-2-0-final.pdf.

Iasevoli, B. (2018, February 15). *Teacher-evaluation efforts haven't shown results, say Bill and Melinda Gates. Education Week.* Retrieved from blogs.edweek.org/edweek/teacherbeat/2018/02/teacher_evaluation_efforts_haven%27t_shown_results_bill_melinda_gates.html.

Jacobs, R., & Kozlowski, S. W. (1985). A closer look at halo error in performance ratings. *Academy of Management Journal, 28*(1), 201–212.

Jordán-Quintero, M. I., Ayala Corredor, C., Cepeda Torres, J. F., Porras Chaparro, C., & Sánchez Arenas, V. C. (2019). Inter-rater reliability in videos of patients with a suspected diagnosis of autism and child psychosis. *Revista Colombiana de Psiquiatría (English Ed.), 48*(2), 80–87.

Kane, T. J., Kerr, K. A., & Pianta, R. C. (2014). *Designing teacher evaluation systems: New guidance from the measures of effective teaching project.* San Francisco, CA: Jossey-Bass. https://doi.org/10.1002/9781119210856.

Kraft, M. A., Brunner, E. J., Dougherty, S. M., & Schwegman, D. (2018). *Teacher accountability reforms and the supply of new teachers.* Retrieved from https://scholar.harvard.edu/files/mkraft/files/kraft_et_al._2018_teacher_accountability_reforms.pdf.

Kraft, M. A., & Gilmour, A. F. (2017). Revisiting the widget effect: Teacher evaluation reforms and the distribution of teacher effectiveness. *Educational Researcher, 46*(5), 234–249.

Lavigne, A. L. (2014). Exploring the intended and unintended consequences of high-stakes teacher evaluation on schools, teachers, and students. *Teachers College Record, 116*(1).

Marzano, R. J., & Toth, M. D. (2013). *Teacher evaluation that makes a difference: A new model for teacher growth and student achievement.* Alexandria, VA: Association for Supervision & Curriculum Development.

Medlock, I. Y. W. (2017). Teacher evaluation ratings and student achievement: What's the connection? (Doctoral dissertation). Available from ProQuest Dissertations and Theses database.

Michigan Department of Education (2019). Michigan educator evaluations at-a-glance. Retrieved from www.michigan.gov/documents/mde/Educator_Evaluations_At-A-Glance_522133_7.pdf.

Nevada Department of Education (2020). Nevada educator performance evaluation system (NEPF). Retrieved from www.doe.nv.gov/uploadedFiles/ndedoenvgov/content/Educator_Effectiveness/Educator_Develop_Support/NEPF/EducatorNEPFProtocols.pdf.

Paige, M. A., Amrein-Beardsley, A., & Close, K. (2019). *Tennessee's national impact on teacher evaluation law & policy: An assessment of value-added model litigation. 13*(2), 52.

Porter, J. M. (2010). Performance assessment for California teachers (PACT): An evaluation of inter-rater reliability. (Doctoral dissertation, University of California, Davis). Retrieved from https://search.proquest.com/education/docview/757340264/abstract/75FB88EFA4754C47PQ/5.

Sergiovanni, T., & Starratt, R. (2007). *Supervision: A redefinition.* New York, NY: McGraw-Hill Education.

Saunders, W. M., Goldenberg, C. N., & Gallimore, R. (2009). Increasing achievement by focusing grade-level teams on improving classroom learning: A prospective, quasi-experimental study of Title I schools. *American Educational Research Journal, 46*(4), 1006–1033.

Schmoker, M. (2012, August 28). Why complex teacher evaluations don't work. *Education Week*. Retrieved from www.edweek.org/ew/articles/2012/08/29/02schmoker_ep.h32.html.

Stecher, B., Holtzman, D., Garet, M., Hamilton, L., Engberg, J., Steiner, E., Robyn, A., Baird, M., Gutierrez, I., Peet, E., Brodziak de los Reyes, I., Fronberg, K., Weinberger, G., Hunter, G., & Chambers, J. (2018). *Improving teaching effectiveness: Final report: The intensive partnerships for effective teaching through 2015–2016.* RAND Corporation. Retrieved from www.rand.org/pubs/research_reports/RR2242.html.

Wolf, R. (1973) How teachers feel toward evaluation. In E. House (Ed.), *School evaluation: The politics and process* (pp. 156–168). Berkeley, CA. McCutchan.

Zepeda, S. J., & Jimenez, A. M. (2019). Teacher evaluation and reliability: Additional insights gathered from inter-rater reliability analyses. *Journal of Educational Supervision, 2*(2), 11.

Faulty Assumptions

As states changed teacher evaluation laws and policies in response to Race to the Top, little discussion took place regarding what the new system already assumed. There is an urgent need for this discussion. Schools are complex systems, with complex programs—and, as we've seen, teacher evaluation systems are among the most complex. The more complex the system is, the more assumptions it involves (Nkwake, 2013). These systems are used to make high-stakes decisions involving hiring, firing and compensation. Ignoring the assumptions that underlie our teacher evaluation programs can be detrimental to the intended outcomes and bring about unintended outcomes and consequences. We need to reimagine how we evaluate teachers through the lens of proven educator engagement, professional learning communities, teamwork and inquiry, and work to become learning organizations.

A Foundation Built on Sand

The faulty assumptions involved in assessing teacher effectiveness have infiltrated our profession like a computer virus, tainting all that we do, digging us into a deep hole of less than impactful programs, actions and theories. In order to create a teacher evaluation program that will produce the intended outcomes of professional and student learning, the assumptions that our current system is built upon must be examined. Without proper examination of stated and implicit assumptions, change cannot occur. "A plan based on faulty assumptions is not likely to bring about the desired goal" (Nkwake, 2013, p. 45). We must examine the assumptions and change them as appropriate in order to have the desired impact on behavior and actions.

The past twenty years of educational reform have focused on raising student achievement for minorities, special education students and students from low-income households, and on increasing college and career readiness. High-quality teaching and employing high-quality teachers is a more recent reform effort implemented with the federal government's involvement via Race to the Top funds available through the American Recovery Act. The funds provided by the federal government encouraged states to redefine high-quality teaching and redesign their teacher evaluation systems. However, little has changed in the area of teacher evaluation. Teachers and principals are frustrated and confused, while student achievement remains stagnant.

All performance evaluation systems are built on assumptions. Those assumptions can be stated or unstated, explicit or implicit. In order to bring about progressive change to any program, the implicit assumptions must be made explicit. After the assumptions have been recognized, they must be evaluated. Do the assumptions contribute to achieving the desired outcomes of the program? If the answer is no, new assumptions must be developed, stated and reflected upon in light of the program's desired outcomes.

There is confusion regarding the purposes of teacher evaluations. It has been stated that there are two purposes of teacher evaluation, formative and summative, or measurement of effective teaching and professional development. A system built on measuring teacher quality will look very different from a system focusing on professional learning (Marzano, 2012; Papay, 2012). Based upon the stated purpose, varying assumptions take hold. Teacher evaluations have struggled with adhering to the two purposes simultaneously. The two purposes interlock and create a tension between what needs to happen and what happens. In the case of teacher evaluations, the systems do not measure the most impactful actions teachers can undertake to increase student learning. Yet we continue to use evaluations to measure effective teaching. The problem is compounded by the need for schools to use evaluation as a professional growth opportunity, hence the dual purpose. The problem is, what if the construct we are seeking to measure is not impactful in terms of the desired outcomes? If that is the case, what are we learning to do as a result of those measurements?

That brings us to the central question: is teacher evaluation available to measure and assess teaching, or is the purpose of evaluation to promote professional learning? These dual purposes have been hard to explicate in policy and practice. "We have erroneously spent a century thinking that evaluators control improvement. Evaluators do not control improvement. Teachers do" (Hazi, 2018, p. 201).

Case Study: An All Too Common Story

At Parkside Elementary, school is three weeks into session. The kids have settled down, the teachers are in a groove and Mrs. Rees, the principal, must begin her formal observations of teachers—and soon, because each teacher needs at least one observation each quarter. After each observation, Mrs. Rees is required to meet face-to-face with the teacher to discuss what she saw. School has just started, but Mrs. Rees is already up against the teacher evaluation clock.

One of the first to be observed is Mr. Samuels, a second-grade teacher. As Mrs. Rees looks on, students ask higher-order questions, enthusiastically discuss the text and write down their thoughts. Mrs. Rees knows by experience and research that the environment in the classroom will have an impact on student learning. After all, Mr. Samuels has been one of Mrs. Rees' best teachers for the last 10 years. After 40 minutes, Mrs. Rees leaves Mr. Samuels' room.

Mrs. Rees makes her way to the room of Mrs. Hernandez, a second-grade teacher in her third year of teaching, still trying to find her place. Mrs. Rees thinks Mrs. Hernandez has potential, but needs to work on engaging the students, a skill that would help her manage the classroom more effectively. Mrs. Rees observes for 40 minutes, takes notes regarding some areas to improve in student engagement and classroom management as well as some positives that she saw, and moves on to a third-grade classroom.

While Mrs. Rees is observing the third-grade teacher, the second-grade team has a collaboration meeting. Mrs. Rees is unable to attend because she is busy observing. This is a frustrating situation for Mrs. Rees. The third-grade team at Parkside has always been very strong. Mrs. Rees sees little need for her to observe all third-grade teachers for 40-plus minutes.

Mrs. Rees would love to facilitate the second-grade team collaborations and help them analyze data, create action plans, talk about student needs and ultimately lead them to a shared understanding of effective teaching. She knows her presence there is needed. Beyond that, Mrs. Rees thinks

Mr. Samuels could be a guide for Mrs. Hernandez. Mrs. Jones thinks she could mentor Mr. Samuels and help him build the confidence he needs to help Mrs. Hernandez grow professionally—a move that would help both teachers.

Mrs. Rees would love to schedule her observations around collaborations, as she did last year. But there are only so many hours in a day. After meeting with teacher teams and conducting individual observations and conferences, when is Mrs. Rees supposed to meet with parents, central office staff and community members? So, like many principals, Mrs. Rees has simply fallen into a mode of compliance, observing teachers, holding the face-to-face conferences, filling out rubrics and writing narratives of observations. The deep collaborative instructional conversations she yearns to have with her teachers rarely take place. She is wasting her and her teachers' time, wallowing in the teacher evaluation muck.

Perhaps the story of Mrs. Rees is why we do not witness school improvement or successful initiatives on a large scale. The current trend of teacher evaluation systems in this country are killing the power of instructional leadership and professional learning for teachers and principals because the system has faulty assumptions. Principals are drowning in compliance with these systems and teachers are driving themselves crazy trying to receive the best "score" possible. Neither way of thinking will help foster the environments schools need to move forward.

> Reward-and-punishment, or carrot-and-stick accountability programs, are not the answer to school underperformance, and the research is very clear on this fact.
>
> (Lassiter, 2012, p. 3)

Principals observing teachers and leading them to improvement is flawed. Using principal observations as the main activity to improve schools does not make any sense in light of relevant research on teamwork, PLCs and collective efficacy. The PLC process creates shared responsibility, understanding, goals and objectives. "Today's schools don't need 'instructional leaders' who attempt to ensure that teachers use the right moves. Instead, schools need learning leaders who create a schoolwide focus on learning both for students and the adults who serve them" (Dufour and Mattos, 2013, p. 39). We need new processes and new assumptions to rebuild our systems that focus more on learning and development and less on measurement.

> The culture in which this work takes place is what separates the high- from low-performing schools. In order to leverage the full potential, we must move away from carrot and stick accountability programs and tap into the intrinsic desire to teach.
>
> (Lassiter, 2012, p. 8)

Faulty Assumptions

> It is not enough to change strategies, structures, and systems, unless the thinking that produced those strategies, structures, and systems also changes.
>
> (Senge, 1999, p.15)

The system is broken because of faulty assumptions. If we could only change the assumptions that dictate the teacher evaluation narrative, we might have a glimmer of hope in creating a system that will produce the desired results of increased professional learning and increased student achievement.

Faulty Assumption #1: Education Should Mimic the Business World

The teacher evaluations in this country mirror the failed systems of small businesses and corporations alike. We assume that because another industry or sector of our economy is doing something, schools should try it as well. We see it in our top-down authority structures, data analysis, peddling students as products and the attitude whereby students are seen as a test score and not a human.

The business world has its moments, but it also has aspects that frustrate and infuriate those who deal with it—think of the cable company you mentally curse after an hour on hold trying to find out why service is down. Or that company you went through three interviews with, only to receive a form letter two months later saying you didn't get the job. A business is "efficient" if it cuts costs and saves time, even if customers and employees alike are fed up. That's not the attitude we want in schools.

One-size-fits-all HR policies and evaluation forms can be a bad fit even in a workplace where everyone is an adult and behaves relatively predictably. Our "customers" are as young as 5. Why would leaders, legislatures or educators want our systems to reflect the same failed systems used in the corporate world? I cannot think of any reason why a method or strategy used in supply chain management or advanced manufacturing, or any other industry, would translate into a fluid, nuanced, critical, unpredictable profession, such as teaching. Why would high-stakes evaluations from the business world translate successfully to education?

I recently had a conversation with a friend who is an operations manager at a family attraction. We were discussing how managing the attraction and being a school administrator can be similar. Our conversation eventually made its way to performance appraisals. His dismay with the performance appraisal process in his company is similar to that of educators. He commented that his company has 12 competencies that every employee must be evaluated on. He recently applied their system to a cashier at the on-site gift shop. As the manager of the attraction, all he needs from his gift shop cashier is to keep the cash drawer balanced and have exceptional customer service. The employee or the manager does not need a hefty list of competencies, standards or behaviors that may or may not be crucial to the success of the position. The goals are very simple: happy customers and a balanced cash drawer.

The manager and the employee would be better served focusing on those two aspects of the job. The manager would be better off communicating those two broad goals while developing systems and procedures with the employee to meet them.

If a cashier is shaky on math, puts change in the wrong place or doesn't know how to handle an angry customer, receiving a low score on an evaluation won't help.

The evaluation isn't the same thing as procedures to have a balanced drawer or good customer service techniques.

We do the same thing in education. We need teachers to collaborate and exhibit collective efficacy. Instead of evaluating them on those two comprehensive goals, we try to measure a teacher's ability to implement prescribed standards and methods that have proven to meet those goals in a setting that may or may not be similar to their own.

A performance evaluation should be concerned with broad goals; the methods, programs and techniques should not be what is evaluated. There is an endless amount of ways to meet objectives— we need professional teams that can set their sights on broadly constructed goals and develop a sensible plan to meet those goals together.

Schools are not a business. They cannot and should not be run like a business, and normal business principles may or may not apply to schools. Schools are a human service industry. Schools cannot crank out numbers, charts, scores, growth points, rates, scales or any other quantification of success. The numbers will tell, at best, half of the story. We work with students, teachers, parents, the community at large, which translates into an unimaginable number of variables and variations to quantify.

Of course, we can use sound practices from other areas, such as accounting practices, facilities management, custodial engineering and more. But only as needed—not as part of a wrongheaded attempt to run a school like a business. If we are going to implement theories and practices from thinkers outside of the education field, we should borrow the concept of the learning organization as presented by many organization thinkers, such as Peter Senge. The learning organization theory started to gain momentum around the same time that schools were beginning to implement PLCs.

The idea of using methods from outside of education to solve education problems as a default strategy has proven to be dangerous, as we see with high-stakes testing and high-stakes teacher evaluations. Schools must lead the way in creating learning organizations. Then the business world can copy us.

Faulty Assumption #2: Principals Should Conduct Classroom Observations of Teachers to Determine Effectiveness

The second faulty assumption forms the foundation of the entire evaluation process: that evaluations of teacher effectiveness should be based on having the principal observe them teach. It sounds reasonable, but it's probably the leading cause of ineffective teacher evaluations.

Principal observations have a long history in teacher evaluations. As outlined in Chapter 1, this line of thinking has been part of our appraisal systems from the beginning. The practice took a firmer grip with the movement to make principals "instructional leaders" starting in the early 1990s. A simple search in ERIC for "principal observations" starting in 2001 yields 1,605 queries. Race to the Top required principals to conduct multiple observations of teachers in a calendar year.

Observing teachers is not ineffective in and of itself. Teachers should be observed, and they should be given feedback. The really good teachers will use that feedback to get even better. The problem is that the whole system rests on observations made by the principal, and those observations are the determining factor in a teacher's rating.

Policymakers seem to place great faith in principals' ability to evaluate a good lesson, stamina to conduct multiple observations on every teacher, and skill to produce reliable evaluations for all the teachers in the building. Perhaps principals appreciate the vote of confidence. However, most administrators are not that good, or simply don't have time. Search for professional books on teacher evaluations, and most of what you will find are self-help programs for principals to manage their schedule and find the time needed to implement evaluations in a school. Other works focus on having critical conversations with teachers explaining how their rating was calculated. They are riddled with protocols for teacher goal setting, focused on narrowly improving a particular skill listed on the rubric, such as "Checking for Understanding."

Some texts and programs focus entirely on managing the documentation component of teacher evaluation systems. In fact, it has become almost impossible to implement one of these teacher evaluation systems without dedicated software and data storage capabilities. The workshops and programs rarely focus on teaching and its improvement: "Evaluation training focuses on the instrument" (Hazi, 2018, p. 200). We're spinning our wheels, not improving teaching or providing growth opportunities.

One person observing a teacher conducting a lesson in isolation is not an effective way to assess teacher effectiveness. It encourages individualistic success in a profession that requires collective efficacy. Teaching is a team sport.

Basing performance evaluation on one person's observation is especially problematic because all performance evaluations are subjective. Time and time again in the literature of performance evaluations, scholars have concluded that all performance evaluations are subjective. Measuring teacher skill is difficult. Evaluators risk biasing the results based on their personal feelings toward a teacher. Additionally, an evaluator may emphasize a skill that he or she values while downplaying another skill that he or she does not. The true quality of a teacher's performance cannot be accurately evaluated using a system that uses the observations of one person.

With teacher evaluations, we have done a good job of making the subjective objective—or so we think. Inter-rater reliability is near impossible. As we discussed in the previous chapter, inter-rater reliability, in multiple fields, is very low—when two or more people observe and rate a characteristic, they frequently rate it differently, even when provided with a clear rubric to base their rating on.

The chance that a principal observing a teacher will provide an evaluation that every skilled observer would agree with is about equivalent to the chance of a basketball player making a full-court shot—it might happen, but it's very unlikely. But we've staked our chances of improving our schools on the chance of making that full-court shot every time. If we had taken the time to develop good processes, we could have had a great chance at a layup.

The body of literature on this subject confirms the idea that this practice is not effective. Firestone et al. (2019) found that the effects of principal observations of teachers are weak. Principals' observations of teachers have little to no effect on their instructional improvement. Lavigne (2014) found that there is no evidence that high-stakes teacher evaluations can improve teacher effectiveness. There is limited research to support the improvement of teaching through principal observations. The vast amount of research has taught us two things: most teachers are rated effective and student achievement is not increasing, even after evaluation reforms have been implemented. Teachers are begging for a more inclusive evaluation system. Principal observations are dreadful for the principal and even more so for the teacher. "There's something deeply personal about appraisals of our teaching," Minkel (2018) has stated. "It's not just our professional competence that's wrapped up in an observation, but a sense of our worth as human beings." The intended purposes of principal observations have not been well served in practice. Teachers dislike them and principals have a hard time navigating the human consequences. Minkel, a former Arkansas Teacher of the Year, deducted that educational administrators can improve observations by focusing on student engagement and creativity, rather than on narrow, less impactful actions such as "the obedient inscription of every lesson's objective on the board" (Minkel, 2018).

Principals themselves can reflect on this assumption—how much impact do your observations have on the instructional quality of your school? If you're like most, you'll say observations have little to no impact.

We're using up our precious time on low-impact actions. Teaching by its very nature cannot be standardized—it is fluid and requires creativity and adaptability. A collaborative conversation with peers has more impact on the improvement of teaching practice than principal observations.

Faulty Assumption #3: Teachers Demonstrate Effectiveness Alone in Front of a Classroom

This assumption is the flip side of faulty assumption #2. We assume that teachers working in isolation from other educators, with students in the classroom, most effectively demonstrate their effectiveness. This belief encourages teachers to work in isolation and does not encourage a collaborative environment based on teamwork.

It's not that collaborative cultures cannot be established under these conditions. Collaborative cultures do exist—but despite our evaluations, not because of them.

Teachers preparing to validate their effectiveness in this manner waste time every year. A principal observing a lesson can assess the effectiveness of that lesson. But the principal cannot assess the overall effectiveness of the teacher based on that observation. Effective teaching is broader than just the interactions that happen in the classroom. This intuition has been confirmed by recent research regarding collective efficacy, collaboration and professional learning communities.

Teaching is a nuanced profession. An infinite number of programs, strategies, methods and techniques have proven effective. What matters is a teacher's ability to perform within the context of local teacher teams, researching and implementing methods based on the needs of the local students through collaborative processes. Teachers most certainly can demonstrate part of their effectiveness by being observed by an administrator. However, this cannot be separated from the collaborative process, interactions between teachers and interactions between teachers and principals. Otherwise, there is no context to assess the collective efficacy of the staff.

We know from research that the most important factors in teacher professional learning and student achievement are collaboration and teamwork—the existence of a professional learning community.

Collective efficacy has been shown to be the number one factor in student achievement, even more important than socioeconomic status (Goddard et al., 2000). The most influential factors that define teacher effectiveness happen outside the classroom. Yet, the element we place the most weight on when evaluating teachers is their ability to deliver a lesson and manage a classroom.

Case Study: Timing is Everything

Mrs. Jackson was a second-year teacher at a large middle school in the Midwest with approximately 1,300 students. She had a successful first year as an eighth-grade language arts teacher. She reflected on her year and felt very confident going into her second year. She knew she still had a lot to learn, but her summative evaluation was good, and her students were successful on the state assessment. She also developed great relationships with her students and families.

At the start of her second year Mrs. Jackson was ready to take the next step in her development. Her principal had mentioned in her evaluation that she needed to improve her questioning of students. As she planned her lessons and consulted with other teachers, she felt confident that she was providing critical questions for students to consider when analyzing a text. The first three weeks of school went great. Students were participating more, asking and answering questions, and collaborating to understand a variety of texts in different contexts. They seemed excited. Mrs. Jackson was pleased with her progress as a professional.

Mrs. Jackson approached her principal, Mrs. Lewis, and let her know that she had taken her advice from last year regarding questioning and that things were going great. Mrs. Lewis was happy to hear that and told Mrs. Jackson that she would be in the within the next couple weeks to observe.

In the meantime, Mrs. Jackson added two new students to her class: twins, Jaylen and John, from another state. She had never known any twins, let alone had them in one of her classes. She was excited about having them in her class but began to notice some subtle differences in the twins as time went by. Jaylen was emotional, distracted, disengaged from classwork. Mrs. Jackson was able to develop a rapport with the troubled student. Although he wasn't the easiest to teach, she appreciated his personality, sense of humor and care for others. Mrs. Jackson had done an adequate job minimizing Jaylen's outbursts and using proactive strategies to calm him down. After all, she cared about Jaylen. She wanted what was best for him.

Four weeks later, Mrs. Lewis came in to see how Mrs. Jackson was doing with questioning techniques. Mrs. Lewis did not get to see what she had hoped for. Instead she saw Jaylen on one of his worst days, and Mrs. Jackson spending time keeping him engaged. Several other kids took advantage of her distraction by talking and playing games, and Mrs. Jackson had to scramble to keep them engaged as well, something she usually did not need to do. Mrs. Lewis wrote in her observation notes that Mrs. Jackson "needs improvement" in classroom management.

Mrs. Lewis was not at the team meeting that resulted in Mrs. Jackson attempting a new behavior intervention she had strategized with her team. She couldn't be at every class, so she couldn't see how Jaylen reacted to the conventional classroom management techniques the rubric prescribed, what his behavior had been when he first arrived, and how it had improved in the weeks since.

A story like this happens in every school, at least once every year, if not more. The consequences of an exchange like the one between Mrs. Jackson and Mrs. Lewis can ripple through the entire building. Not only did Mrs. Lewis tear down a new teacher, she dismissed Mrs. Jackson's entire team, who collaborated with her to try the new intervention. All for what?

This narrative is not a critique of the teacher, team or principal. This is a critique of the system that teachers and principals are required to navigate, and the negative consequences of that system. In its current form, it perpetuates fear, fear of failure, and discourages the initiative to try.

Faulty Assumption #4: Teacher Evaluation Rubrics Must Incorporate As Many Characteristics of Effective Teaching As Possible

Another assumption that sounds logical but doesn't work holds that teacher evaluation rubrics should incorporate as many characteristics of effective teaching as possible.

Prior to the Race to the Top reforms in 2009, teacher evaluation documents usually had a few descriptions of teaching elements, each with a box to rate the teacher's performance as 1 ("low"), 2 ("on target"), or 3 ("above target"). Each state or district had its own terms, but the general premise was the same. Some documents also called for principals to rate teachers as unsatisfactory vs. satisfactory or effective vs. ineffective, linked to a statement regarding teaching. Most of these documents were just a few pages long and left little, if any space, for a narrative.

Fast forward to the 2010s. After Race to the Top, all states developed new teacher evaluation rubrics and systems. Some teacher evaluation documents are 15–45 pages long, with hundreds of bullet points describing effective and ineffective practices. The professionals using the tools are unable to find agreement on the definition of the terms used within, so state departments of education (such as the Colorado Department of Education) are foolishly attempting to ensure inter-rater reliability by defining them. Educators spend hours upon hours defining and arguing over terms and concepts in hopes of conclusively determining what is effective or not.

State agencies and even private companies have taken the 15–45–page documents and developed manuals of implementation that can reach hundreds of pages. We've gone from one extreme to the other—if the two-page carbon copy sheets were minimal, we've now switched to multi-page documents highlighting hundreds of concepts.

The types of strategies, programs and activities teachers can implement to impact student achievement are endless. I suppose someone thought they could write it all down and then attempt to hold teachers accountable. But this is a poor attempt at stand-ardization of effective teaching. The more teaching strategies we mandate teachers use, the less freedom they have to use their intelligence and employ strategies that work in the context of their classrooms.

Hazi (2018) has noted that the evaluation documents tell us more about who created the document than about the teacher being judged by the tool. For example, the framework for teaching presented by the Danielson Group (Danielson Group, n.d.) assumes a constructivist approach to teaching. Is a constructivist approach to teaching always the best method? Of course, not. Danielson is a self-proponent of constructivism. I adhere to constructivist philosophy myself. But what if the unit being taught or the lesson being delivered was not inten-tionally constructivist? What if the day's lesson required, for good reason, a more behavioralist approach?

High-quality teaching must be defined at the local level, considering the local needs of the teachers and students through collaborative processes. Standardizing teaching to a checklist or bullet points is a troubling practice. Teachers and principals should be using teaching frameworks as a resource to solve local problems, not as inflexible rules. Otherwise, a school runs the risk of focusing on issues that really are not issues for them; their time and effort is wasted, and they do not move forward to solve the problems the surveys were intended to address.

Case Study: Positive Deviants

Mr. Craig was an elementary principal at a hard-to-staff school with societal challenges. High teacher turnover and high poverty created unique challenges for the staff to overcome, but overcome them they did! As one of the highest student-growth schools in the state, they were able to use their collective knowledge and efforts to improve at a rate higher than most schools in the state. That year, they showed moderate gains in achievement but great gains in student growth. The students did not necessarily achieve state-level benchmarks, but they learned and showed that learning through high levels of content standard growth.

It all started in a collaboration with his fifth-grade team very early in the school year. The team, consisting of the teachers and instructional coach, came to Mr. Craig with a set of math data and their anecdotal observations. Their observations and data showed a few skill and concept gaps that were having a negative effect on most students' overall math performance. They developed a plan and tracked their own data. He gave the teachers until October 1st to fill the gaps. By October 1st, the gaps were filled, and they were rolling! They had tremendous math and ELA growth—near the top in the state.

This situation could have gone a different way. At the beginning of the year, they had a 15-page teacher evaluation rubric, 83-page school improvement plan, curriculum protocols and scripted intervention plans. They had to make a decision. Implement programs that didn't fit the needs of their school, or collaborate to identify, prioritize and implement strategies that their kids needed. Mr. Craig sat down with his leadership team and told them,

> The first thing we are going to do is forget about evaluations. Don't even think about it. I will talk to teams and individuals if I see a problem. If you see a problem, talk to me so we can action-plan support for teams or individual teachers. No one in this school needs to think about evaluation or worry about what their evaluation will look like at the end of the year.

Saying that requires a certain level of trust and belief in the vision and mission of the school. The staff had great relationships and they were able to agree not to worry. But that's not the case in most schools. In fact, they were positive deviants. Maybe they got lucky. There was certainly a risk that they would be criticized (or worse) if they ignored the 83-page plan and then didn't get the results they wanted. But why should they have had to sidestep all of this just to do what's best for our kids? Mr. Craig did know this—they followed the correct processes to put them, and most importantly their kids, in a position to be successful.

Common Teachers

Teacher evaluation documents, protocols and rubrics have encouraged the development of common teachers. By common, I mean standardized, generic, uniform. But good teaching is anything but standard. Research on teacher effectiveness has focused on the wrong processes, if one can even call them that. The strategies, techniques and behaviors that are accepted as "research-based" are not even processes in a contemporary sense.

Processes in today's organizations need to be redefined as collaboration and collective inquiry in order to choose, prioritize, implement, assess and adjust actions or practices. The process that needs to be evaluated isn't the way a teacher explains a worksheet or disciplines a student for being disruptive, but the work of the team and individual contribution to the success of the team. We don't need any more research on teacher behaviors that constitute effectiveness other than in terms of their performance and engagement in a professional learning organization.

Teacher evaluation has become a predictable yet dysfunctional ritual: a classroom visit, announced or unannounced, followed by a conference. In the current accountability movement states have attempted to fix this century-old ritual with a rubricated, research-based instrument, and by adding more measures, metrics and infrastructure. These additions give the public, policymakers and educators the impression that we have made progress, when we have not. They have complicated rather than substantively changed the practice.

Faulty Assumption #5: Effectiveness Is Defined by Classroom Teacher Actions, In the Moment, In the Classroom

The idea of using research to find the best ways to reach students sounds great. What could go wrong? In fact, it's behind another dangerous fallacy: that teachers must employ a cadre of "research-based" instructional strategies during a lesson to demonstrate their effectiveness.

In today's schools, evaluation isn't just an afterthought for teachers choosing the techniques they find most effective. They're required to use the evaluation documents to help them align their own instructional practices with research. The expectation is that teachers use the documents to learn about strategies, implement strategies and show evidence of effectiveness. The rubrics focus on items such as checking for understanding, asking higher-order questions, not allowing students to opt out, delegating time between parts of a lesson...the list could go on for pages.

Teachers should not be evaluated on their ability to perform these tasks, but on how and why they choose to use them.

Defining effective teaching in an evaluation rubric will lead to limited, idiosyncratic definitions of effective teaching (Hazi & Rucinski, 2016). As a result, educator professional development will focus on adherence to the rubric and the state's definition of quality, not necessarily the impact of the actions of the professionals. The strategies and research in the documents may not be applicable to the context of the teaching and learning taking place, causing more confusion and incoherent definitions of success and failure.

Using research is not a bad thing—we know a lot about effective teaching. But that knowledge is not useful unless incorporated in the context of student learning. And the time taken up by quantifying adherence to the research is itself detrimental to teaching. "In addition to being inconsistent with current research on student learning, these restricted definitions of teaching lead to increased checklists, walkthroughs, and increased specificity of procedures and instruments" (Hazi & Rucinski, 2009, p. 12).

A bad idea that's "research-based" is harder to get rid of then one that's based on intuition or habits. The "research-based" nature of the strategies in evaluation lend a perceived legitimacy to the whole evaluation process. Teachers and principals can defend their actions by evoking the term "research-based." When a teacher is not living up to the descriptors in a rubric, a principal can evoke the "research" to criticize them. And a teacher who's using research-based strategies can defend themselves, even if their students aren't thriving.

Using or promoting a strategy that is research-based has an appeal of security. It has become a crutch for our profession—creating the illusion that we have been more effective or made more progress than we have (Hazi, 2018). And while it appears to ground our approach in scientific inquiry, it has actually taken professional inquiry out of the process. Instead of relying on each other—our fellow teachers and principals—we have relied on findings from studies done in places we've never been to by people we've never met. We think that by implementing them, we will produce the desired results. But the methods outlined in the rubrics are often implemented outside of the local context and not done collaboratively. They may have worked for the educators who did the study but produce boredom or disengagement in our classrooms.

Demanding specific teaching techniques also lowers the accuracy of observations—which are already questionable. When teachers are being observed, they scramble to conduct what is demanded on the rubric instead of what they usually do, no matter how effective. They're not using the research on effective teaching as it was intended—as a collaborative resource to solve problems. The rubrics and all of their research end up inhibiting the collaborative process. And the principals who observe these classes may have no idea what techniques actually contributed to the successes and challenges of a given classroom over the course of a year.

Teachers should not have to attempt to conform to a rubric with dozens of "effective" strategies in a culture of compliance. They should be given the freedom to discuss the steps needed to increase student learning with their peers and implement what has been discussed and decided upon without fear. The current system is overloading, tiring and confusing for teachers. An effective system would encourage teachers to analyze the current situation, brainstorm ideas with their peers and implement what they decide upon in a collective manner.

Faulty Assumption #6: Document, Document, Document

Teachers believe it is necessary to document all of their positive qualities, because if they don't....an administrator will use one of these ridiculous evaluation tools to find something wrong with their performance and they will lack proof to argue for a better rating. This isn't the way to achieve deep, authentic professional growth.

If teachers don't like having to over-document, principals aren't happy either. Principals are concerned with how teacher evaluations affect school culture. The formality and fear factor with evaluation is too great in the profession right now. The system creates a barrier or a wall of mistrust and lack of confidence in people's intentions. Principals are worried about the amount of time and energy required to document observations in these systems.

Teachers and principals end up playing a dirty game of lawyering to uphold a perception of fairness, rigor, hard work, feedback and productive activity, all in the name of effectiveness. The ironic aspect of all these antics is that they have nothing to do with student achievement, as the RAND Corporation reported in the Bill and Melinda Gates Foundation's Measure of Effectiveness (MET) project (Stecher et al., 2018).

Our teacher evaluation systems do more harm than good to increase adult professional learning and student achievement. Teachers and principals focus on minute points, instead of the broad beliefs, behaviors and concepts that lead to school improvement. We do not need all these documents and narratives to improve schools, professional learning or student achievement. What we need is more educators to sit down and talk, have a conversation, ask questions, seek understanding and knowledge; we need educators to learn from one another, not document lessons or proficiency levels on narrow-pointed strategies that may not even fit the needs of the school. If teachers are following basic collaborative and PLC principles, they will grow in their profession without needing a stack of paperwork to prove it.

If a teacher is unable or unwilling to perform in a PLC then a principal can start documenting for legal purposes, not because the documentation will help that teacher improve in and of itself. The normative process for teacher improvement is in collaboration with their peers and principal, in a face-to-face meeting. Teacher improvement is a process-oriented endeavor, not one of documentation. We have to drive out fear from our organizations. Reducing fear means building relationships, making teachers feel that help is available and those around them trust their judgement. Our documentation is destroying trust.

The time eaten up by documentation could be used for regular, more frequent conversations (Lin & Kellough, 2019). This change could both gain back some of the lost time and make evaluation more accurate by giving principals deeper knowledge of what teachers are doing.

The rubrics currently in use provide a narrow window for administrators to look for effective teaching, ignoring the most impactful actions teachers can take to improve student learning. We need rubrics systems that evaluate processes, not isolated actions. Such systems would take into consideration that the profession is complex and requires the use of experience, using data and context to implement effective instruction tailored to schools' local needs.

Faulty Assumption #7: Carrot and Stick Are the Best Motivators

If a visitor from outer space with no knowledge of human culture read a typical U.S. teacher evaluation form, they'd likely conclude that teachers are a lazy group of people who would do little on the job unless compelled to. After all, why else provide a long list of tasks and grade them on how regularly they're doing them? That's not reality, but it is the basis for perhaps the most erroneous belief of all: that teachers are not motivated to improve on their own. In this worldview, teachers need an administrator to encourage their improvement through formal evaluation systems.

Education researchers Robert Dufour and Mike Mattos, in a 2013 article in *Educational Leadership*, made a case with striking similarities to mine. The authors attempted to uncover the logic of the teacher evaluation reforms. They noted teachers' recognition of the ineffectiveness of evaluations and ask sarcastically, "So why not make tougher evaluation of teachers a cornerstone of school improvement? Why not require principals to spend more time in classrooms supervising and evaluating teachers into better performance? (DuFour and Mattos, 2013, p. 35)."

The assumption of these reforms is that teachers are not motivated to improve student learning and must have a prize or punishment waiting for them. "We can find no research to support the assumption that educators choose to use mediocre instructional strategies and withhold effective practices until they receive increased financial incentives" (DuFour and Mattos, 2013, p. 39). This practice also confers on principals the role of enforcer—making sure teachers work as hard as they should.

This is also linked to the performance pay debate. I do not believe that teachers need to be threatened into improvement. I also do not believe that teachers are willingly refusing to incorporate the best strategies to meet students' needs. Almost all teachers come to work with the best intentions in mind and want to do well for their students. If a teacher is lacking some skill and does not seek improvement, then that teacher is in the minority. Teachers are naturally intrinsically motivated to do well at their jobs. We have placed the demand to drive teacher improvement on the administrators. It is time we place the demand for teacher improvement on the teachers themselves. I also think that teachers would rather have it that way. The erroneous belief that teachers are not motivated, and that they need a carrot or stick waved in front of their faces to improve, is not only flatly wrong, it is insulting.

The argument for teacher evaluation reform is that the public deserves to know the quality of their schools. Throughout this reform and debate, I don't recall parents pushing for high-stakes anything, let alone an evaluation system that would dehumanize and demoralize their child's teacher or see their own child's success peddled like a product.

There's one assumption we can make with confidence: that teachers, principals, students and their parents all want the same thing, effective education that helps kids grow and flourish. The energy and will to achieve this are there among teachers. If they're channeled in the right way (and not into time-wasting forms), we can achieve remarkable things. In the next chapter we will look at traditional definitions of high-quality teaching and seek to redefine the term, to be more inclusive and to move toward collective efficacy.

Tips and Talking Points

Examine the Assumptions that your Organization Holds for Evaluations

Educating children cannot happen in a vacuum. Root methods do not move a first- or second-grade student from learning to read to reading to learn. There is much to be learned from quantified, scientific methods to teaching. However, at the end of the day, we are in the human services industry. There is no prescribed method that works in every classroom, school or lab. We have methods that work in a general sense, but nothing can account for the distribution of variables that our students bring to us every day. They are human beings that must be nurtured, cared for, and *known* by the ones leading them. The same is true for teachers. Collaborative structures, relationships and good old-fashioned teamwork are the only methods that work 100% of the time. We need to stop standardizing and prescribing good teaching. We need to tap into teachers' inherent desire to help students learn and be part of a collaborative team. The individualistic modes of the past have come and gone, and did not anyway truly have a positive impact on student learning. Our teachers deserve better, and our kids deserve better.

Inter-Rater Reliability

Avoid systems that emphasize inter-rater reliability. A study of note from the health care industry (Chow et al., 2016) found that inter-reliability of screenings is difficult in theory and practice. The California teacher evaluation system was the subject of this study (Porter, 2010) and find inter-rater reliability did not exist. Zepeda & Jimenez (2019) reported mixed conclusions for inter-rater reliability finding that there was adequate overall reliability, but disagreement between high and low performers. Jordán-Quintero et al. (2019), reported their findings of video inter-rater reliability study involving autistic child patients. Here was their conclusion, inter-rater reliability was weak. They also encouraged the idea of evaluating children with serious conditions as an interdisciplinary team, to compensate for partial assessment of a patient's psychological abilities. Aoki et al. (2019), studied inter-rater reliability of assessment for the diagnosis of oral cancer. There was no inter-rater reliability amongst nurses and nurses and doctors. The list of study after study trying to find a way to establish inter-rater reliability continues. A limited number of studies have been able to establish inter-rater reliability in any field, not just education. This is a result of misusing terms, definitions and research. Measurement of teaching is not the same as evaluation. Measurement of teaching has its rightful place in professional development, but it does not have a place as the primary means for assessing a teacher's overall effectiveness. Inter-rater reliability is scarce in education as in other industries.

Value-Added Measures

Avoid systems that focus on "value-added measures." VAMs (value-added measures) are an important policy initiative to note: I do not want to spend a lot of time on the subject, because this work is about the observation of effective teaching. However, VAMs received a considerable amount of attention as a result of Race to the Top. Alongside the new observation rubrics and the requirement for principals to conduct multiple teacher observations, VAMs were also required.

Researchers Paige, Amrein-Beardsley and Close (2019) investigated VAMs in policy, practice and law. They found teachers had mixed success in fighting these measures in evaluation systems across the country. The courts, when upholding their use legally, did question the wisdom of such actions. The researchers made it a point to mention that VAMs are not valid or reliable statistically. Yet their use continues to this day in almost every state in the Union.

References

Chow, R., Chiu, N., Bruera, E., Krishnan, M., Chiu, L., Lam, H., DeAngelis, C., Pulenzas, N., Vuong, S., & Chow, E. (2016). Inter-rater reliability in performance status assessment among health care professionals: A systematic review. *Annals of Palliative Medicine, 5*(2), 83–92.

DuFour, R., & Mattos, M. (2013). How do principals really improve schools? *Educational Leadership, 70*(7), 34–40.

Goddard, R. D., Hoy, W. K., & Hoy, A. E. W. (2000). Collective teacher efficacy: Its meaning, measure, and impact on student achievement. *American Educational Research Journal, 37*(2), 479–507.

Hazi, H. M. (2018). Coming to understand the wicked problem of teacher evaluation. In S. J. Zepeda & J. A. Ponticell (Eds.), *The Wiley handbook of educational supervision* (pp. 183–207). Hoboken, NJ: John Wiley & Sons, Inc.

Hazi, H. M., & Arredondo Rucinski, D. (2009). Teacher evaluation as a policy target for improved student learning: A fifty-state review of statute and regulatory action since NCLB. *Education Policy Analysis Archives, 17*, 5.

Hazi, H. M., & Arredondo Rucinski, D. (2016). Teacher evaluation and professional development: How legal mandates encroach on core principles of supervision. In J. Glanz & S. J. Zepeda (Eds.), *Supervision: New perspectives for theory and practice* (pp. 187–200). Lanham, MD: Rowman & Littlefield.

Lassiter, C. J. (2012). *The secrets and simple truths of high-performing school cultures*. Englewood, CO: Lead + Learn Press.

Marzano, R. (2012). The two purposes of teacher evaluation. *Educational Leadership, 70*(3), 14–19.

Minkel, J. (2018, September 18). The particular agony of teacher observations. *Education Week*. Retrieved from www.edweek.org/tm/articles/2018/09/18/the-particular-agony-of-teacher-observations.html.

Nkwake, A. M. (2013). *Working with assumptions in international development program evaluation*. New York, NY: Springer.

Paige, M. A., Amrein-Beardsley, A., & Close, K. (2019). Tennessee's national impact on teacher evaluation law & policy: An assessment of value-added model litigation. *Tennessee Journal of Law and Policy*, 13(2), 52.

Papay, J. P. (2012). Refocusing the debate: Assessing the purposes and tools of teacher evaluation. *Harvard Educational Review*, 82(1), 123–143.

Senge, P. M. (1999). The dance of change: The challenges of sustaining momentum in learning organizations. New York: Currency/Doubleday.

Stecher, B., Holtzman, D., Garet, M., Hamilton, L., Engberg, J., Steiner, E., Robyn, A., Baird, M., Gutierrez, I., Peet, E., Brodziak de los Reyes, I., Fronberg, K., Weinberger, G., Hunter, G., & Chambers, J. (2018). *Improving teaching effectiveness: Final report: The intensive partnerships for effective teaching through 2015–2016*. RAND Corporation. Retrieved from www.rand.org/pubs/research_reports/RR2242.html.

Teacher Quality, Effectiveness and Evaluation

 ## Excellent Teachers, Excellent Students

Parents, students, teachers, administrators and policymakers have long accepted the linkage between teacher quality and student achievement (National Commission on Teaching and America's Future, 1996; Hattie, 2009). The better the quality of teachers, the better students will perform in the classroom. If a school wants to improve student performance, the most effective step educators can take is to improve teacher collective efficacy (Donohoo, Hattie & Eells, 2018).

An urgent need thus exists to find way to raise teacher quality, and to determine when we have done so. Multiple methods and yardsticks have been proposed, and in some cases codified in law. One potential marker of teacher effectiveness is a professional teaching degree. The No Child Left Behind Act required teachers to obtain an education degree in the area in which they were to teach, and to gain state-level certification or licensing in those areas. Past research has suggested that this decision was correct (Darling-Hammond, 2000; Hawk, Coble & Swanson, 1985; Goldhaber & Brewer, 1999). Multiple studies, as referenced above, have concluded that teachers who earned a degree in education and become certified by their respective states have better student achievement outcomes.

Wilson, Floden and Ferrini-Mundy (2001), in their executive summary to the United States Department of Education, found that teachers are more likely to have a positive impact in the classroom if they have received training in subject matter, instructional and pedagogical methods, learning theories, educational foundations and classroom management. But this does not mean a blueprint exists for the most effective course of education each teacher should follow. The researchers noted that there is a need for more research in these areas, and that the issue is complex because there is not enough definitive research into the level of content knowledge and the types of pedagogical training preservice teachers need most.

Another factor is experience. Kini and Podolosky (2016) noted, in their meta-analysis of teacher experience and teacher effectiveness, that teachers with more experience have a greater impact on student outcomes. As teachers gain experience, they acquire valuable knowledge and build on it from day to day and year to year. Through practice, they learn and become better at their jobs.

Since there are only so many highly experienced teachers, knowing the importance of experience can only do so much to improve the education system. Another factor more within educators' control concerns teaching strategies. Extensive research exists on types of instructional strategies that garner the greatest impact for student success. Marzano, Pickering and Pollock (2001) conducted a meta-analysis of hundreds of research studies to synthesize the available findings regarding effective instruction in the book *Classroom Instruction That Works: Researched-Based Strategies for Increasing Student Achievement*. The authors found that identifying similarities and differences, summarizing and note-taking, reinforcing effort and providing recognition, homework and practice, non-linguistic representations, cooperative learning, setting objectives and providing feedback, generating and testing hypotheses, cues, questions and advanced organization strategies yielded the best results for student learning and achievement. Zemelman, Hyde and Daniels (2005) compiled the best practices available in each content area: reading, writing, math, science and social studies. The authors go so far as to tell the reader what actions to increase and decrease in each subject area to produce the most student gains. The book is a great resource for teachers to use when selecting strategies for their students. However, widespread use of these methods is lacking.

The types of strategies, programs and activities teachers can implement impacting student achievement are detailed in the above-referenced research. But using this knowledge to improve teaching is not straightforward. Teaching effectively is not an exact science; it is a skill, nourished through real experiences, successes and failures. The most effective technique to use in any given situation cannot be objectively determined by consulting the research.

Further, identifying behaviors, strategies, skills and knowledge teachers must acquire and exhibit is not enough to influence student learning. Assessing teachers formally, with a rubric defining high-quality teaching by identifying behaviors and strategies, is not enough either. In fact, it is proving to be very limiting.

Another problem with trying to identify strategies that affect learning is that there are just so many of them. John Hattie, in a presentation to the University of Auckland Australian Council for Educational Research (2003), discussed six areas that contribute to student learning: student, home, school, curricula, teachers and learning approaches. Hattie contended that a student's teacher has the greatest effect on that student's achievement, and reported that most everything schools do to teach students can have a positive impact on student learning and achievement. He then reasons that we must identify and use not just the aspects of teaching that have a positive effect on a student's education, but specifically those aspects that have a *profound* effect on a student's education. Donohoo, Hattie and Eells (2018) released an updated list of the practices that have the most profound effect on student learning. Their report found that the most impactful concept teachers can embrace to increase student learning is collective efficacy—a communal belief in their ability to succeed and effect change. As we shall see later in this chapter, research can offer insights into concrete ways to bolster collective efficacy.

Teaching is a nuanced and complex profession (Danielson, 2007, 2016). The nature of the job makes it difficult to measure quality teaching through research (Hazi, 2018). When research identifies highly effective characteristics, behaviors or actions, subsequent studies often fail to validate the effectiveness of those specific actions.

The answer to this may not be more studies and an endless quest to find results we can replicate. Effective teaching will need to be defined at the local level. Part of the nuance of education is the local context of the school and variables of the students they serve.

The measurement of effective teaching at the national level has caused confusion. The profession has become a conglomerate of randomly placed, narrowly defined aspects of effective teaching, complied with and used by many without regard to context.

Disregarding the context in which the teaching takes place results in bias and the extrapolation of faulty assumptions to programs, strategies and actions that may or may not be in the best interest of the student's academic achievement or well-being. Teacher quality, teacher effectiveness and teacher evaluation have been linked into a false metric resulting in a false narrative of what actually constitutes effective teaching and quality teachers, overlooking what really matters. Our systems have become our own worst enemy.

Some Things are Just Hard to Measure

Basing teacher evaluation on research makes it likely that evaluations will be based on whatever is most easily measured.

Measuring exactly what makes a teacher effective has been difficult. Consequently, administrators are mandated to rely heavily upon observable skill-based evaluations. As we've discussed, most teachers in the United States are evaluated based on a series of observations by their school principal. If an evaluator observes certain predetermined skills commonly exhibited by teachers, that teacher is perceived as a high-quality teacher.

Teacher quality has never been easy to quantify. Recent reforms in education have focused on evaluation of teachers in relation to a set of skills based on a rubric of quality teaching. The core competencies of effective teaching are *knowledge*, *instructional skills* and *collaboration/ teamwork*. I have been arguing that collaboration/teamwork is the most important of these—but it's the most difficult to measure, and so often gets short shrift because of our desire to quantify everything and use metrics to communicate.

It would be nearly impossible for a rubric to include all the ways a teacher can demonstrate his or her effectiveness—and, as we've seen, trying to include them all just makes evaluation worse. In an observational evaluation, rubrics define a predetermined list of behaviors or approaches, thus limiting the scope of teacher influence.

Effective Teaching: A Redefinition

As a research community, we have done a masterful job of measuring minute aspects of effective teaching. The irony in all of this knowledge is that professional learning and experience shows much more promise than throwing darts at random, isolated, research-based constructs. Teamwork and collaboration lacks emphasis in our formal processes and systems. If schools would employ the correct processes, providing professional learning and creative experiences, the known effective strategies would be put to better use in the context in which the professionals find themselves. High-quality teachers and effective teaching are redefined to match the requirements of a successful professional learning community, rather than teachers being seen as individuals performing in isolation.

> Good teaching occurs when educators are involved in a cycle in which they analyze data, determine student and adult learning goals on that analysis, design joint lessons that use evidence-based strategies, are coached and supported in improving their classroom instruction, and then assess how their learning and teamwork affects student learning.
>
> (Killion & Roy, 2009, p. 16)

Viewing effective teaching through the lens of the collective efforts of teams is a new way of thinking about evaluation. It is revolutionary because it is hard to measure, it is contextual and subjective. Attempting to measure teaching quality has led to a de-emphasis of broad constructs, because broad constructs are impossible to quantify. Using rubrics limits teachers' ability to find and use the best strategies for their students. Teachers need the freedom to collaborate and implement the best practices for the context in which they work. They should not have to worry about adherence to a rubric that does not fit the objectives of the school, class or lesson.

Improve Evaluation Systems; Increase Collective Efficacy; Raise Student Achievement

A teacher evaluation system should be linked to proven systems of teacher inquiry, collaboration and program implementation that empower teachers to be instructional leaders. Professional learning communities (PLCs) are among the most promising and proven elements of school culture and practice to fulfill this requirement.

What are professional learning communities? They are teams of professionals, working together to accomplish a common goal. PLCs are collaborative teams that inquire into best practices in their local context, creating new knowledge for a clearer view of reality. PLCs use that knowledge to action plan, strategize, analyze data, meet goals, celebrate, fail, learn and try again.

Saunders, Goldenberg & Gallimore (2009) won an award from Learning Forward in 2010 for their work in researching the effect PLCs have on raising student achievement. Their research evaluated the implementation of a PLC at Title I schools. The schools demonstrated increased achievement over a three-year period and achieved greater student growth as compared to schools with similar demographics that did not implement a PLC.

PLCs and Collective Efficacy

Collective efficacy is one of the strongest predictors of a successful organization. If a school wants to improve student performance, the most effective step educators can take is to improve collective efficacy (Donohoo, Hattie & Eells, 2018; Hattie, 2003). Collective efficacy has a greater effect on achievement than does a student's socioeconomic status (Ross, Hogaboam-Gray & Gray, 2004).

Jenni Donohoo, in her book *Collective Efficacy* (2017), presented a detailed analysis of how a community of educators can work most effectively to serve students. Donohoo defined "collective efficacy" as teachers' communal belief that they can influence student learning and achievement, with six enabling components:

- Advanced teacher influence

- Goal consensus

- Teachers' knowledge about one another's work

- Cohesive staff

- Responsiveness of leadership

- Effective systems of intervention

Donohoo (2017) stated that "Collective efficacy is increased through collaborative learning structures" (p. 54). By contrast, collective inefficacy is cultivated through observations, evaluation cycles, over-analyzation of terms and definitions on rubrics, rating scales, point systems, ranking systems and performance categorizing.

A professional learning community (PLC) is a structured way to ensure that teachers are asking the right questions, collectively solving problems, building cohesion, learning about and from one another, setting goals, spreading their influence and creating learning environments and tasks that meet student needs. Teacher efficacy, collective efficacy, and PLCs are directly dependent upon one another. As Hattie found, collective efficacy is the number one factor in raising student achievement.

When administrators work with teachers and evaluate their ability to work in a PLC, the good teachers will only get better and the poor teachers will quit before any administrator would even have to observe them teaching. Using a PLC evaluation system provides many benefits over traditional teacher evaluation systems at increasing instructional leadership. The district, administration and teachers can benefit from a PLC evaluation system.

In particular, Donohoo has challenged us all to allow teachers to have more influence. After all, if teachers truly drive improvement, we should encourage them to have more influence. Placing the demand for teacher improvement on the administrators will not produce the desired results. Teachers need to be at the forefront of change, driving its planning, implementation and fine-tuning.

Teamwork in Other Industries and Education

PLCs are essentially a way to build and enhance teamwork in a workplace. Why is that so important? Working as a team to accomplish a goal is one of the most satisfying experiences in the human condition. We are wired to be social beings and to solve problems together. We can see this play out in our lives, family, sports, work and neighborhood. But the concept of individual merit has tainted our ability to be our best. We know that together we are better, but the false hope of individualism has skewed our vision for collective success.

Fleisch et al. (2011) reported on a study of schools that have improved and sustained improvement. The authors found that teachers who worked together collectively in a learning organization were able to achieve and maintain achievement. The authors noted that the schools in which teachers worked more in isolation and did not exhibit a capacity for learning were less successful. Teacher collaboration around cultural awareness and proficiency have a positive effect on Black male student achievement (Rodgers, 2016). The positive effects of collaboration and teamwork are abundant in education.

Below are some examples from literature on the power of teamwork. Below I set out a detailed example from the medical industry, where the nurses of Johns Hopkins University Hospital developed collective professional practices and found great success. We have seen similar success in schools with the formation of PLCs, and in other industries and sectors researchers have found similar findings. The following studies and articles, grouped by industry, have demonstrated the benefits of teamwork:

- Business: Teamwork enhances organizational structure, excellence, quality, results, creativity and learning; builds trust, resolves conflicts and creates ownership; reduces stress on individuals (Tripathy, 2018); leadership and teamwork equals success (Henderson, 2017).

- Financial Industry: Team-managed funds outperform individually managed funds (Patel & Sarkissian, 2017).

- Construction: Teamwork produces job satisfaction, safety, effectiveness, successful strategies (Drouin & Sankaran, 2017).

- Government services: Georgia Department of Transportation: trust breeds teamwork, teamwork equals performance (Cho & Poister, 2014).

- Health care: Teamwork increases efficiency, compliance, safety, quality (Rosen et al., 2018). At the Mayo Clinic, "Experience has shown that individuals who pool their resources as a team in pursuit of a common purpose lift the human spirit and generate energy. Teamwork enhances learning as teammates teach each other, and it inspires confidence through camaraderie and encourages extra effort as teammates rely on one another" (Berry & Beckham, 2014).

PLC in Action

Johns Hopkins University nurses developed a professional practice model that is in essence a PLC for nurses, and is a great example of a true learning organization empowering the people actually doing the work. Here are a few of the nurses' quotes from the book-length study of this model by Dang, Rohde and Suflita (2017):

> We have a very professional practice. We try to improve our care each day and improve patient satisfaction. The relentless pursuit of excellence—that's what we're always after in big things and little things, in the details, and in every day.
>
> (Dang, Rohde & Suflita, 2017, p. 7)

> I think it's really important for nursing....to harness each other's strengths.... We work toward interdisciplinary collaborations to really gain a good understanding of who the patients are, what their medical needs are, and what they'll need when they go home.
>
> (Dang, Rohde & Suflita, 2017, p. 8)

> We are given a lot of leeway to speak our minds, advocate for patients and our own practice.... We have a lot of involvement, and that doesn't just impact what nursing does—it also impacts policies for the hospital—and for patient care in general.
>
> (Dang, Rohde & Suflita, 2017, p. 7)

The book's foreword notes the hospital administators' and professional nurses' commitment to "empowering nurses to engage in key decisions about practice and quality of work life; recognizing and celebrating professional development and excellence in clinical practice; and influencing inter-professional, evidence-based care delivery through inquiry and performance improvement" (Dang, Rohde & Suflita, 2017, p. XXI).

The Johns Hopkins model is founded on learning organization principles. The nursing professionals collaborated to develop a model of professional practice, hold each other accountable, and implement the best practices for patient well-being. Their model makes full use of the most powerful resources they have to drive success in nursing practice: the nurses themselves.

This sounds so simple yet feels so revolutionary. The professional practice model requires nurses to continually examine their practice and adapt based on data (quantitative and qualitative), discussions, debates and research. Nurses use the model to improve individual practice and the collective practice of the team. They assume shared governance and emphasize sound leadership practices to encourage collaboration and excellence.

Administrators and nurses work together to set policy and develop procedures and protocols. Nurses collaborate with one another to learn, adapt practice, innovate and create. The broad assumptions lead to the facilitation of behaviors and attributes that encourage teamwork.

There is no doubt what the medical professionals value at Johns Hopkins. Each nurse is empowered to act as a key agent of patient care, collective inquiry and collective efficacy.

In the professional practice model, requirements for nurses are very broad, leaving the in-the-moment decision making to the nurse on the floor, using their knowledge and systems as a guide to make the right decision. The nurses at Johns Hopkins understand that their work is variable, nuanced and unpredictable, and they must rely on and trust one another to make the best decisions for patient care.

Among the most noteworthy element of this system is the fact that the document does not advocate for any particular strategy or program as standard practice. The document establishes its grounding in patient- and family-centered care and counts on the collaborative system to find the right strategies and programs for the situation.

Teamwork in Education: Professional Learning Communities (PLCs)

PLCs are the best, least expensive, most rewarding way to improve schools (Saunders, Goldenberg & Gallimore, 2009; DuFour, DuFour, Eaker & Many, 2010; DuFour & Mattos, 2013; Gallimore, Ermeling, Saunders & Goldenberg, 2009). "But while the term (PLC) has become widespread, the underlying practices have not, and many of the schools that proudly proclaim to be PLCs do none of the things PLCs actually do" (DuFour, DuFour, Eaker & Many, 2010, p. 21). Replacing the old ways of evaluating will change day-to-day life for the better. The new requirement will be to assess and evaluate collective decision-making and good, old-fashioned teamwork. Teachers cannot close their classroom doors and administrators cannot hide in their offices or behind a computer screen, clicking boxes for an evaluation. Teachers and principals must learn to work interdependently, using the evaluation as a tool to drive conversations in the moment, on a daily basis, as part of an intentional meeting, professional learning and mutual exchange of ideas.

Principal and teacher conversations cannot start or end with assessment of teaching as the main topic. Creating the processes will require principals to break from old methods and allow the innovation and creativity of their teams to take over and guide the direction of the school. Principals and other leaders will have to make sure teachers have the conceptual knowledge of PLCs and the skills to function effectively within a PLC.

Specifically, teachers will need to hone the skills of

- Collaborating
- Building effective assessments
- Analyzing data
- Targeted intervention innovation (Ferriter, Graham & Wight, 2002)

Other key actions concern teaching-related tasks, lesson planning, sharing resources for learning-related tasks, strategizing, prioritizing and sharing successes and failures.

Principals also need to ensure a safe learning environment for adults, driving out fear and embracing reflection. Principals and teachers need to learn to reflect on what is and isn't working in their practice, and not be afraid of the results. "Progress-driven leaders must figure out where their schools and their teachers are right now and then focus everyone on taking micro steps that represent progress" (Ferriter, Graham & Wight, 2012, p. 80). Principals must assess their teams to see if they need support in working together as a process or working together to collaboratively accomplish tasks.

Making teamwork work in schools is no easy task. However, as you see, by evaluating our collaborative processes, linked to the best practices of PLCs, we can remove the biggest barrier to establishing schools as learning organizations.

The education system must change. Teachers can no longer be followers or employees who follow directions; they must become leaders of their own learning and leaders in assisting each other in learning. Building a collective capacity for learning, leadership or responsibility starts with changing our processes. Our evaluation processes are not aligned with the most effective means to achieve student learning and growth and adult professional learning. We need systems and structures to guide us through improvement processes. Teaching is no longer assessed by a snapshot of learning in the classroom, but by the educator's ability to engage in self-reflection and formative processes, through collaboration collectively.

Educators have been talking about PLCs for a long time. Some schools are able to tap into the power of PLCs, but some who have tried one have not succeeded. I believe the faulty assumptions and influence of teacher observation practices are a main reason why most schools have not been able to tap into the power of professional learning teams. I do not believe that teachers and principals are purposely sidestepping active engagement in a PLC. Rather educators are sent conflicting messages from our systems on what is important and lean toward concentrating on what they feel they can control: their own evaluation. Dufour and Marzano (2008) have noted that teachers view the PLC process as "a meeting" or a program, not as a way of being and part of the school culture.

Teacher isolation continues in many schools to this day. Teachers are isolated from their colleagues. There are great collaborative schools all over this country, despite our lawmakers' and policymakers' intentions. As long as we are evaluating teachers in isolation, there will always be a focus on the success of the individual teacher, inhibiting the school's growth into a true learning organization. We have tried and tried to change, but the road-block of our isolated systems has proved to be too hard to overcome. This is all the more reason to make our evaluation system into a learning process.

A new evaluation system designed on PLC principles can change our schooling practices. The problem is not that educators prefer to be isolated. Educators yearn to truly collaborate. I have heard educators communicate that they understand the positive effects of collectively building each other's instructional and leadership capacity and the positive effect on student achievement. I have also heard many times that sentiment be followed up with "But what about high-stakes evaluations and high-stakes student assessment?" We know what needs to be done to produce the most student learning gains—we're just trapped doing something different.

The Capable Teachers are Already Here

> The challenge confronting public education is not recruiting more good people to an ineffective system, but rather creating powerful systems that allow ordinary people to achieve success.
>
> (DuFour and Marzano, 2008, p. 19)

One advantage of this approach is that it doesn't require hiring a phalanx of high-performing new teachers. In their book *Leaders of Learning*, Dufour and Marzano (2008) examined school reform efforts over the past thirty years. Among the items that keep reappearing is "Recruit capable people." As the authors pointed out, though, it is not that simple.

United States public school teachers are an educated, caring group of people who are highly motivated to help kids succeed—messages from politicians that blame them for our school systems' problems miss the mark. We already have the workforce we need to achieve a great education system.

Recruiting good people into a broken system will fix nothing: "The effort to bring qualified people into the field must be accompanied by a concerted effort to make the profession more satisfying and fulling" (DuFour & Marzano, 2018, p. 19). The profession can be more fulfilling if the system can harness the collaboration, problem-solving, creativity and innovation that people desire. If we continue to hand things down to people, no one will want to work in a school because the professional, innovative culture they desire to participate in is becoming non-existent in schools. If we don't change, it might be too late. The workforce demands are already weighing down districts across the country. We have great teachers in every school. It is time we harness their innate, learned and potential abilities.

 # Teachers Are Already Collaborating—Sometimes

It's not that teachers don't work collectively already. It's just that that work is rarely part of any official policy or system. But it is striking that the most effective means we have available to improve schools are used only as informal processes. Collaboration and being a part of a team—and functioning within that team to grow and help others grow—is sadly reduced to informal adherence to effective practices.

We cannot tell teachers to work as a team and collaborate when we evaluate then mainly on what happens when they are in front of the kids, in isolation. We cannot tell them to be collectively responsible for student learning and then, the only time they receive feedback, have it come from one person who just watched them teach with no other teachers in the room. As long as we try to function in this mode, the only successful schools will be positive deviants.

 ## The Learning Evaluation

PLCs can become a part of our school cultures, in just the same way that observations, feedback and annual performance reviews have dominated our cultures, actions, behaviors and thinking for so long. What better way to implement the PLC process than to assess the process itself as a formal endeavor?

The traditional structure of our schools is one of isolation. Principals find it hard to influence the growth of 30-plus people all at once. A PLC evaluation would allow principals to work with teacher teams in a close, intimate environment. The principals could facilitate the direction of the teams and build consensus and cohesion around common goals and objectives. This structure also influences shared leadership. Principals will need impactful contributors to school teams: teachers who have distinguished themselves as leaders, who influence others and can focus a team on the problem or task at hand. A PLC evaluation encourages teacher leaders. By evaluating how teachers lead and engage in collaborative processes, a principal will be able to identify who his or her teacher leaders are, in addition to identifying high-quality teaching. It is the only way to know.

A principal cannot know who their teacher leaders are by watching them teach. Principals must observe how teachers interact in their teams to assesses who the leaders are in the group. A PLC evaluation makes principals capacity builders in the open. In a PLC evaluation, a principal can stop wasting time observing teachers and start using that time to facilitate collaborative processes. Dufour and Marzano in their book called continually for principals to enact the strategies needed to build PLCs and capacity. However, the current system does not afford most principals the capacity to do that, even if they wanted to.

Teacher quality is explicitly linked to teamwork, more than any individual action, behavior or characteristic of a teacher. Teachers that have time to collaborate and are provided structures to inquire can solve any problem. Principals need to be a support piece for the teacher teams in moving forward. Principal support and facilitation for clarity of work are essential if a school is to be a learning organization.

Dufour and Marzano (2008) offer seven strategies for implementing PLCs:

- Put together meaningful teams
- Give them time to collaborate
- Provide support structures for growth
- Clarify the work for the teams
- Monitor the work and provide direction
- Avoid shortcuts
- Celebrate wins and confront those who do not contribute

These are straightforward, common-sense strategies to get PLCs started in any school. Particularly important in any evaluation system are support structures, clarity of work, monitoring of the work and confronting non-contributors. All teachers need support, and their ability to receive and give support to make collective changes should be evaluated carefully.

Principals and teacher leaders will always need to clarify what needs to be done—that is the role of leaders. However, if after many clarifications a teacher still does not get it, that can be evaluated negatively. By monitoring the work and providing clarity, principals can assess a teacher's capacity to work within a team and use that new knowledge to make changes in their teaching. This too can receive more emphasis in an evaluation. A PLC doesn't mean less rigorous evaluation—rather, it means closer scrutiny for those educators who are either unable or unwilling to contribute to the team. Closer scrutiny, that is, but also more support. A learning evaluation is about support, teamwork and learning together.

Do Teacher Dispositions Still Matter?

A body of literature exists highlighting teacher dispositions as seen from a university training and human resources perspective. University preparation programs have used dispositions as part of their accreditation programs since the 1990s (Freeman, 2007), and are required to assess teacher dispositions (Council for the Accreditation of Educator Preparation, 2013).

Our focus on the measurement of teaching seems to have put teacher dispositions in the past. That might be a mistake. In this measurement era we must not lose sight of elements already established in research. Researchers have noted the role that dispositions play in teacher quality (Altan, Lane & Dottin, 2019) and are in agreement that dispositions, along with knowledge and skills, are important to effective teaching and the study of effective teachers. But the topic has been subject to its own vagueness.

Are teacher dispositions innate or learned? Fonsec-Chacana (2019) has set out the traditional definition of dispositions: "dispositions are personal and interpersonal attributes that people display in professional contexts" (p. 268). The ambiguity of the term and definitions create tension within the research community. To minimize confusion, the author offered a new definition of teacher dispositions: "the cultivatable set of intellectual, intrapersonal, and interpersonal attributes that enact teacher knowledge and skills to the service of a professional community, which includes students, student families, and other education professionals" (p. 268).

Teacher dispositions are both inherent and taught. In the context of a learning community, a teacher can learn about himself or herself and align his or her knowledge, skills and beliefs with the goals of the organization.

What Does This Mean for Us?

The idea of such a radical change in evaluation can raise concerns for everyone involved in education. Teachers may worry that they're being scored on alien or unpredictable criteria, while parents and other citizens may jump to the conclusion that this communal, subjective system would take the rigor out of evaluation. In the sections below, I address some logistical questions about evaluation.

Is negative evaluation necessary?

The ugly side of any managerial or administrative position is the act or process of ending a person's employment. While some television shows have treated firing as a joke, any compassionate leader has never taken such matters lightly, and certainly does not take joy in changing the trajectory of an individual's life by ending their employment, in education or any industry.

Most teachers are striving to be their best, learning and growing with varying degrees of effectiveness. Ideally, teacher evaluation systems would be eradicated, and people would learn through collaborative structures that they are not cut out for the work and simply choose to do something else. But we don't live in a utopia. Just as in every other professional field there are individuals who do not behave morally, ethically or legally, and there are just a few individual teachers who are simply incompetent. Teacher evaluation systems are necessary in order to address severe incompetence.

Evaluation systems are not needed from a legal standpoint to dismiss teachers for immoral, unethical or illegal behavior. School boards in every state have the ability to dismiss teachers legally under such circumstances through due process. But they are needed if a teacher is to be terminated for poor performance.

One of our nation's founding principles is the right to due process. We all have this right, and that should include the right of an employee to be evaluated using a transparent, fair process and appeal any unjust termination. Due process is a right guaranteed by the 14th Amendment to the U.S. Constitution. While teacher dismissal policies differ from state to state and between different court rulings, the underlying philosophy is that there must be documentation of deficiencies, an opportunity for the teacher to improve (documented) and documentation that the teacher was unable to improve.

Abolishing performance evaluations for teachers would leave the legal system unable to rule on legal matters when a teacher does need to be dismissed. That should not deter us from creating a system that evaluates those aspects of teaching that matter most.

Teachers that are able to be impactful contributors, learning to contribute to teams, and teachers that are limited in their contributions should be able to learn without fear or retribution. We need to begin about ways we can differentiate teachers who are impactful or le be impactful from those who are simply unwilling. Those that are unwilling to contribute to the collective processes would have these issues noted in their evaluations as a serious problem. They would be moved out of the Learning Evaluation system and into a new system to comply with legal requirements.

Conclusion

Working together as part of a collaborative team is the only way to assess teacher effectiveness impactfully. High-quality teaching is contextual. The advancement of teaching is related to educational professionals' abilities to define high-quality teaching in a collective framework and to collaborate in finding the best methods to teach their children. Therefore, I am proposing a teacher evaluation system that assesses teachers according to their ability to participate effectively in a professional learning community, as opposed to an observational teacher evaluation system that focuses on individual adherence to a rubric.

The profession is always changing. Methods go in and out of fashion. Best practices seem to come and go with the changing policies handed down to schools. New technology enters our lives and classrooms. Kids' interests, home lives and post-school plans certainly aren't what they were a century ago. And we've adapted to it all. If the Covid-19 pandemic has shown us anything, it is that our public schools are adaptable, and teachers are ready and willing to do whatever it takes to serve students and families. Since the NCLB Act, public schools have been in a state of change and uncertainty.

Still, some aspects of education have remained the same for decades. When one looks back at John Dewey's work, it's striking that some of the same systematic and cultural practices he lamented remain in effect today: desks, rows, school structure, grade levels, degrees, certifications, all the way up to large-scale traits like the isolation of teaching. But there's another constant: the need for teamwork. Through research we are sure of one thing: teacher collaboration and principal facilitation of that collaboration garners the most student learning.

It is my contention that the most effective teachers are able to participate in and contribute to a learning organization, and that this ability more strongly influences student learning than any knowledge or instructional skills they may possess or acquire. It is also my contention that by participating in a learning evaluation, teachers will be able to learn new skills or acquire new knowledge more effectively than if schools continue to evaluate teachers as they have for the decades.

A strong connection should exist between the items that are included in a rubric and what we know about effective teaching; the behaviors included should be those that most strongly influence student success. Every school is different and has different needs. In a Learning Evaluation system, teachers and principals work together to identify, select and implement the best strategies and programs tailored to meet the needs of their students. Therefore, I am proposing an evaluation system that will assess teachers' ability to contribute to the collective efficacy of the school through the implementation of a learning evaluation.

Numerous skills, strategies and pedagogical approaches are effective. It would be nearly impossible to include all the ways a teacher can demonstrate their effectiveness in a rubric. In an observational evaluation, rubrics define a predetermined list of behaviors or approaches, thus limiting the scope of teacher influence. Implementing effective teaching strategies and evaluating teachers is disconnected. Every school is different and has different needs. The need for individual, standardized observation-based rubrics and evaluations has passed.

Tips and Talking Points

Student-Centered Observation Rubric

Introduced here is the Student-Centered Observation Rubric. Teacher teams can use this as a formative tool to provide each other feedback on the most important aspect of high-quality teaching, the skills, behaviors and actions of the students.

What students are *actually* doing during today's lesson is both the source of and yardstick for school improvement efforts.

(Moss and Brookhart, 2012, p. 12)

If we're radically reshaping how we observe and evaluate teachers, won't that affect how we observe students? The answer is yes—we'll be observing them more closely and insightfully.

Our efforts in school improvement and teacher effectiveness have focused on the wrong people. First, teacher improvement has become mainly an administrative task. Second, we have sought to overanalyze what the teacher is doing, to comply with a rubric, and have neglected the actions of the people we are trying to influence, the students. It is the students themselves that should serve as the formative influencers in designing and implementing learning targets and experiences. After all, they are the ones whom we are trying to help gain insight, understanding and knowledge.

Where students are and where they need to be should be the driver of instruction, planning and assessment. Students should also be one source of data to determine effective teaching. We defined effective teaching as a collaboration process earlier. Now we are defining effective teaching's *results*. The results are what the students are actually doing in the room. Focusing our attention on students during an observation will give teacher teams valuable information to learn, adapt, adjust and change to meet student needs. Implementing the best teaching practices is meaningless if the students themselves are not affected impactfully.

Want to spot an effective teacher? Watch the kids! The use of rubrics focusing on teacher behaviors has failed to shine a light on a very important aspect of learning: the students themselves. It is more valuable to observe a classroom and watch the students than the teacher. Students who are engaged with impactful instruction exhibit certain behaviors and modalities. Effective teachers engage students, clarify purpose, support productivity and stimulate student collaboration and inquiry. The student-centered observation rubric establishes a foundation for teachers to think about the results of their collaborative work as professionals. The rubric centers on broad themes, highlighting general attributes of students that are learning.

Each element of the rubric is highlighted by a graphic (see Figure 4.1) outlining the assumptions of the student actions and how they come to life in the classroom.

Student Centered Observation Rubric

Indicators	Evidence Observed			
Indicators	**Impactful Contributor**	**Learning to Contribute**	**Inconsistent Contributor**	**Non-Contributor**
Student Engagement	Student inquiry is a normal aspect of learning in the classroom. Learning opportunities connect students' culture, personal concepts and ideas, which motivates and excites them about learning. Real-world application of concepts occurs organically for students.	Teacher is learning to engage students in meaningful work through students' backgrounds, identities, processes of inquiry and inquisitiveness. Students have opportunities to inquire but require teacher direction. Real-world application of concepts occurs in the learning environment but requires teacher direction.	Teacher inconsistently engages students in meaningful work due to teacher directed models of instruction and influence over curriculum and pedagogical practices. This creates a learning environment that inconsistently applies to the real world for students.	Teacher-directed instruction dominates the pedagogical practices in the classroom. Students answer more questions than they ask and rarely have opportunities to inquire.
Purpose	Students consistently understand what is expected of them and they know what they are learning and why. Students use feedback to progress in meeting lesson objectives, purposes and/or goals for learning tasks. Learning opportunities link to real-world experiences for students.	Teacher is learning to establish clear lesson objectives, purposes and/or goals for learning tasks. Teacher is learning to provide students with feedback. Students are learning to make real-world connections to the concepts they are learning.	Learning activities sometimes lack purpose, clear objectives and goals. Lessons sometimes do not connect to students' lives, resulting in a disconnection from the real world and student personal experiences.	Real world application of learning is lacking in activities and lessons. Rote learning and passive learning dominate pedagogical practices in the classroom establishing a lack of real-world purpose to learning.
Productivity	Students consistently produce and present quality work in different contexts: written, orally, digitally and/or through publication. Produced work answers real life questions, solves real life problems, encourages better questions and continues the work of inquiry.	Students are learning to consistently produce and present quality work in different contexts: written, orally digitally and/or through publication. Teacher is learning to facilitate processes of inquiry to foster student curiosity. Students are learning to engage deeply in learning to solve real life problems, ask questions and inquire.	Students are inconsistent in the variety of production in the classroom. Teacher is attempting to facilitate the production of student work in various contexts. However, students revert to paper-and-pencil or traditional methods more often. Student inquiry is limited and lessons are teacher-directed at the wrong times.	Students are consistently engaged in traditional modes of producing work, and providing evidence of learning via paper and pencil, closed questions, quizzes and tests.
Student Collaboration	Students' collaboration leads to student engagement in real world activities. Students collaborate to create and produce quality work in varying formats. Students collaborate to present and display work in varying formats. Student collaboration leads to curiosity and inquiry. Students collaborate to ask open questions, solve real world problems, create solutions and discover knowledge.	Teacher is learning to facilitate student collaboration, increasing student engagement, learning, production and processes of inquiry.	Student collaboration is not a normal or consistent avenue for student learning, production, inquiry and discovery of knowledge. The teacher leads students through content more often than than students collaborate and inquire together.	Students rarely, if ever, have an opportunity to collaborate, solve problems, ask questions or discover knowledge. Teacher-directed pedagogical practices are consistently used to deliver content to students.

Figure 4.1 Student-centered observation rubric

Observation of Student Outcomes

Engagement

> Engagement could be described as the holy grail of education.
>
> (Sinatra, Heddy & Lombardi, 2015, p. 1)

Turner and her colleagues (2014) have stated that "how classroom participants act together can support students' value for learning as well as their beliefs that they can be successful, their willingness to engage, and how related they feel to others" (p. 1197–1198).

Effective teachers find a way to engage students through collaboration. Students can become engaged in learning through an endless bank of strategies, resources and programs. Through the work of collective inquiry teachers find the best possible way to engage and motivate students based on the objectives, learning targets and goals. They will connect with students on a human level. Teachers embrace diversity and make learning real for students from different cultures and backgrounds. Teachers take the time to learn about their students personally, academically and behaviorally. Teachers consider the background of students when providing learning opportunities in a real-world context.

There is no limit to the impact that engagement has on the educational attainment of students. Student engagement has been linked to achievement and learning (Fredricks et al., 2016), meaning (Lemov, 2010) and positive behavior (Fredricks et al., 2016). Teachers at the local level should themselves be collaborating to define engagement for their classrooms and

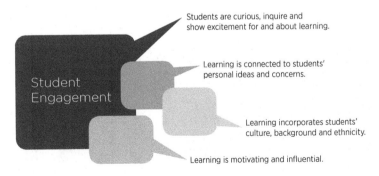

Figure 4.2 Student engagement

school. By discussing and agreeing upon the definition of student engagement, teachers can begin to look for their own areas of improvement to increase engagement in their school.

Purpose

> The most effective teaching and the most meaningful student learning happen when teachers design the right learning target for today's lesson and use it along with their students to aim for and assess understanding.
>
> (Moss and Brookhart, 2012, p. 2)

A classroom with purpose is one that connects the experiences in the room with the real world. The students themselves know how to ask questions and research answers. Students know how to formulate questions to solve problems. There is genuine ambition to be creative and innovative. Students understand expectations and provide feedback to each other and receive impactful feedback from the teacher. Students and teachers tackle issues and problems together and develop understanding that leads to increased inquiry.

Student purpose spans lessons, units, assessment, activities and experiences. Without purpose, or a target, true understanding and learning is extremely difficult to attain (Moss and Brookhart, 2012). Purpose in a classroom is linked to long-term learning goals. Students understand what, why and how they are to learn in a room that encourages trial and error, and use the culture of the room to establish personal purposes through feedback and opportunities to progress.

Purpose

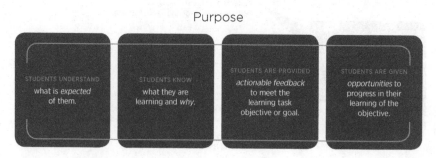

STUDENTS UNDERSTAND what is *expected* of them.

STUDENTS KNOW what they are learning and *why*.

STUDENTS ARE PROVIDED *actionable feedback* to meet the learning task objective or goal.

STUDENTS ARE GIVEN *opportunities* to progress in their learning of the objective.

Figure 4.3 Student purpose

Productivity

Student productivity should not be confused with productivity as a person might normally think of it in the context of economic activity. Ultimately, student productivity will guide students to ask more questions. It's similar to high-quality research. Good quality research leads to more questions, because knowledge is discovered or created, and leads to further questions of improvement and progress. Student productivity is no different. Student collaboration leads to accomplishment and increased inquiry, which is productive. Productivity increases inquiry, collaboration and problem solving. Productivity is never the end. It is just the beginning.

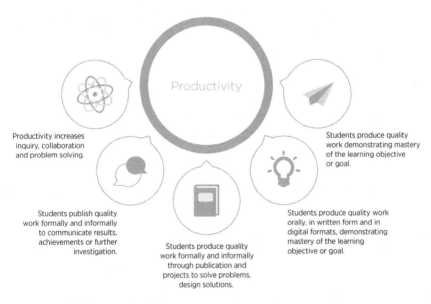

Figure 4.4 Student productivity

Student Collaboration

Student collaboration has the potential to dramatically increase student learning. Student collaboration has been linked to increasing students' ability to think critically, and to increased interest and motivation (Mosley et al., 2016). In collaboration students develop a positive demeanor toward

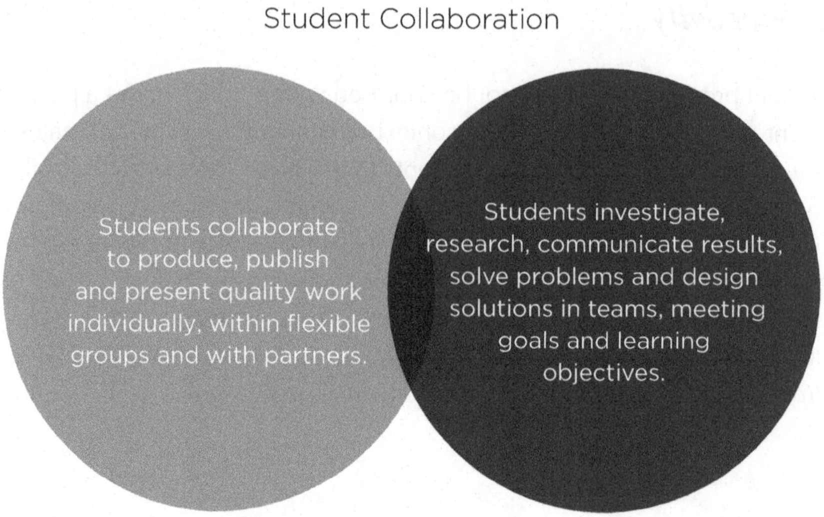

Student Collaboration

Figure 4.5 Student collaboration

each other and to academics, and try harder (Roseth et al., 2008). Student collaboration and true engagement are linked. Students that collaborate are more engaged, care about their learning more and are motivated to grow as learners. When students are engaged in collaborative efforts they find it easier to progress through difficult tasks and learn in a supportive environment (Jansen, 2012).

The benefits of productive student collaboration are endless. By focusing on what the students are doing, principals, through the facilitation of collaborative teams, can encourage collaboration with teachers around the best possible way to engage the students that they serve.

Positive Relationships

The ability to influence positive relationships with students and amongst students is absolutely critical for effective teaching and learning to occur. Teachers that are effective have students that respect the teacher and each other. Students are invested in the success of the classroom as a unit. Fear of failure is driven out of the room and students feel safe. There is genuine love and care for all persons in the classroom community.

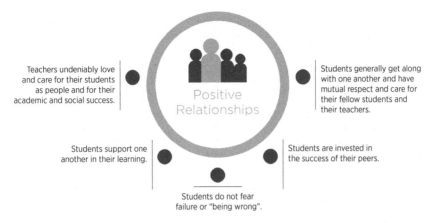

Figure 4.6 Positive relationships

Student-Centered Observation Rubric (SCOR)

The SCOR is a tool for principals, teachers, teaching teams and anyone else who wants to peer into a classroom and observe students. Classroom observations shift from observing the teacher to observing the students. This makes sense. If I want to get a full picture of a dance teacher's ability, I go watch her pupils perform. If I want to assess an elementary teacher's reading teaching ability, I go listen to the students read. Comprehensive teacher actions lead to effective student practices. The rubric is used as a formative tool in conjunction with the learning evaluation. It is a tool to assess teacher impact in the classroom as a result of the work done in teacher teams.

References

Altan, S., Lane, J. F., & Dottin, E. (2019). Using habits of mind, intelligent behaviors, and educational theories to create a conceptual framework for developing effective teaching dispositions. *Journal of Teacher Education, 70*(2), 169–183.

Berry, L. L., & Beckham, D. (2014). Team-based care at Mayo Clinic: A model for ACOs. *Journal of Healthcare Management; Chicago, 59*(1), 9–13.

Council for the Accreditation of Educator Preparation. (2013). Standards. Retrieved from; www.ncate.org/standards/introduction.

Cho, Y. J., & Poister, T. H. (2014). Managerial practices, trust in leadership, and performance: Case of the Georgia Department of Transportation. *Public Personnel Management; Thousand Oaks, 43*(2), 179–196.

Dang, D., Rohde, J., & Suflita, J. (2017). *Johns Hopkins nursing professional practice model: Strategies to advance nursing excellence.* Indianapolis, IN: Sigma Theta Tau.

Danielson, C. (2007). *Enhancing professional practice: A framework for teaching* (2nd ed.). Alexandria, VA: Association for Supervision & Curriculum Development.

Danielson, C. (2016, April 20). Charlotte Danielson on rethinking teacher evaluation. *Education Week.* Retrieved from www.edweek.org/ew/articles/2016/04/20/charlotte-danielson-on-rethinking-teacher-evaluation.html.

Darling-Hammond, L. (2000). Teacher quality and student achievement. *Education Policy Analysis Archives, 8*(0), 1.

Donohoo, J. (2017). Collective efficacy: How educators' beliefs impact student learning. Thousand Oaks, CA: Corwin.

Donohoo, J., Hattie, J., & Eells, R. (2018, March). The power of collective efficacy. *Educational Leadership, 75*(6), 40–44.

Drouin, N., & Sankaran, S. (2017). *Project teams and their role in organizational project management.* Cambridge, UK: Cambridge University Press.

Dufour, R., DuFour, R., Eaker, R., & Many, T. (2010). *Learning by doing: A handbook for professional learning communities at work.* Bloomington, IN: Solution Tree.

DuFour, R., & Mattos, M. (2013). How do principals really improve schools? *Educational Leadership, 70*(7), 34–40.

DuFour, R., & Marzano, R. J. (2008). *Leaders of learning: How district, school, and classroom leaders improve student achievement.* Bloomington, IN: Solution Tree.

Ferriter, W. M., Graham, P., & Wight, M. (2002). *Making teamwork meaningful: Leading progress-driven collaboration in a PLC at work.* Bloomington, IN: Solution Tree.

Fleisch, B. (2011). Mona Mourshed, Chinezi Chijioke and Michael Barber: How the world's most improved school systems keep getting better [Review]. *Journal of Educational Change, 12*(4), 469.

Fredricks, J.A., Filsecker, M., & Lawson, M.A. (2016). Student engagement, context, and adjustment: Addressing definitional, measurement, and methodological issues. *Learning and Instruction, 43*, 1–4.

Freeman, L. (2007). An overview of dispositions in teacher education. In M. E. Diez & J. Raths (Eds.), *Dispositions in teacher education* (pp. 3–29). Charlotte, NC: Information Age.

Fonseca-Chacana, J. (2019). Making teacher dispositions explicit: A participatory approach. *Teaching and Teacher Education, 77*, 266–276.

Gallimore, R., Ermeling, B., Saunders, W., & Goldenberg, C. (2009). Moving the learning of teaching closer to practice: Teacher education implications of school-based inquiry teams. *The Elementary School Journal, 109*(5), 537–553.

Goldhaber, M. and Brewer, D. (1999). Does teacher certification matter? High school certification status and student achievement. Unpublished manuscript.

Hattie, J. (2003). Teachers make a difference: What is the research evidence? Melbourne, Australia: Australian Council for Educational Research: Annual Conference on Building Teacher Quality.

Hattie, J. (2009). *Visible learning: A synthesis of over 800 meta-analyses relating to achievement*. London; New York: Routledge.

Hawk, P. P., Coble, C. R., & Swanson, M. (1985). Certification: It does matter. *Journal of Teacher Education, 36*(3), 13–15.

Hazi, H. M. (2018). Coming to understand the wicked problem of teacher evaluation. In S. J. Zepeda & J. A. Ponticell (Eds.), *The Wiley handbook of educational supervision* (pp. 183–207). Hoboken, NJ: John Wiley & Sons, Inc.

Henderson, T. (2017). Leadership and teamwork: The secret sauce to business success. Forbes Coaches Council. Retrieved from www.forbes.com/sites/forbescoachescouncil/2017/02/08/leadership-and-teamwork-the-secret-sauce-to-business-success/#4eca9c5736f1.

Jansen, A. (2012). Developing productive dispositions during small-group work in two sixth-grade mathematics classrooms: Teachers' facilitation efforts and students' self-reported benefits. *Middle Grades Research Journal, 7*(1), 37–56.

Johnson, S. M. (2019). Where teachers thrive: Organizing schools for success. Cambridge, MA: Harvard Education Press.

Killion, J., & Roy, P. (2009). *Becoming a learning school*. Oxford, OH: National Staff Development Council.

Kini, T., & Podolsky, A. (2016). Teaching experience and teacher effectiveness. *American Educator, 40*(3), 3.

Lemov, D. (2010). *Teach like a champion: 49 techniques that put students on the path to college.* San Francisco, CA: Jossey-Bass.

Lewis, L., Parsad, B., Carey, N., Bartfai, N., Farris, E., Smerdon, B., & Greene, B. (1999). *Teacher quality: A report on the preparation and qualifications of public school teachers.* Washington, DC: National Center for Education Statistics.

Marzano, R. J., Pickering, D. J., & Pollock, J. E. (2001). *Classroom instruction that works: Research-based strategies for increasing student achievement.* Alexandria, VA: Association for Supervision and Curriculum Development.

Mosley, P., Ardito, G., & Scollins, L. (2016). Robotic cooperative learning promotes student STEM interest. *American Journal of Engineering Education, 7*(2), 117–128.

Moss, C. M., & Brookhart, S. M. (2012). *Learning targets: Helping students aim for understanding in today's lesson.* Alexandria, VA: Association for Supervision and Curriculum Development.

National Commission on Teaching & America's Future (Ed.). (1996). *What matters most: Teaching for America's future: Report of the National Commission on Teaching & America's Future* (1st ed.). New York, NY: National Commission on Teaching & America's Future.

Patel, S., & Sarkissian, S. (2017). To group or not to group? Evidence from mutual fund databases. *Journal of Financial and Quantitative Analysis, 52*(5), 1989–2021.

Rodgers, J. O. (2016). *Successful strategies for educating Black males in English language arts.* [Doctoral dissertation, University of West Georgia].

Roseth, C. J., Johnson, D. W., & Johnson, R. T. (2008). Promoting early adolescents' achievement and peer relationships: The effects of cooperative, competitive, and individualistic goal structures. *Psychological Bulletin, 134*(2), 223–246.

Rosen, M. A., DiazGranados, D., Dietz, A. S., Benishek, L. E., Thompson, D., Pronovost, P. J., & Weaver, S. J. (2018). Teamwork in healthcare: Key discoveries enabling safer, high-quality care. *American Psychologist, 73*(4), 433–450.

Ross, J. A., Hogaboam-Gray, A., & Gray, P. (2004). Prior student achievement, collaborative school processes, and collective teacher efficacy. *Leadership and Policy in Schools, 3*(3), 163–188.

Saunders, W. M., Goldenberg, C. N., & Gallimore, R. (2009). Increasing achievement by focusing grade-level teams on improving classroom learning: A prospective, quasi-experimental study of Title I schools. *American Educational Research Journal, 46*(4), 1006–1033.

Sinatra, G. M., Heddy, B. C., & Lombardi, D. (2015). The challenges of defining and measuring student engagement in science. *Educational Psychologist, 50*(1), 1–13.

Tripathy, M. (2018). Building quality teamwork to achieve excellence in business organizations. *International Research Journal of Management, IT and Social Sciences, 5*(3), 1–7.

Turner, J. C., Christensen, A., Kackar-Cam, H., Trucano, M., & Fulmer, S. M. (2014). Enhancing students' engagement: Report of a 3-year intervention with middle school teachers. *American Educational Research Journal*, 51(6), 1195.

Wilson, S., Floden, R., Ferrini-Mundy, J. (2001). *Teacher preparation research: Current knowledge, gaps, and recommendations*. Seattle, WA: University of Washington Center for the Study of Teaching and Policy.

Zemelman, S. (2005). *Best practice: Today's standards for teaching and learning in America's schools /*. Porstmouth, NH: Heinemann.

5

Dawn is Here
A New Day for Educators

> No single approach will be effective in every situation, for each set of instructional purposes, or with all individuals or groups of students. These choices and decisions represent the heart of professionalism.
>
> (Danielson, 2007, p. 24)

Teaching is not a one-size-fits-all endeavor. We can construct a system that gives teachers the latitude to attempt multiple approaches to teaching and learning based on the needs of the school, their classroom and students.

Allowing flexibility and abandoning false assumptions doesn't mean turning teaching into a free-for-all with no structure. Instead, the new system is built on a few broad assumptions.

In the previous chapter we explored the faulty assumptions of our current system. In this chapter we will explore what the new assumptions could entail and how those new assumptions can influence more impactful behaviors demonstrated by principals and teachers.

Falling Between Two Purposes

As we saw in Chapter 4, the two purposes consistently stated for teacher evaluations are summative (accountability) and formative (professional learning). School leaders are trapped between these two purposes (Lillejord & Børte, 2019). Why do many teacher evaluation systems fail to achieve this dual purpose?

Broad Assumptions of Teacher Efficacy	
Motivation	Teachers are intrinsically motivated to help students
Teamwork	Educators solve problems with teamwork
Collective Efficacy	Educators are interdependently linked to the success of the organization
Context	The local school culture, community needs, institutional knowledge and cultural proficiency are prioritized in the organizational objectives and goals
Collective Inquiry	Educators have processes that influence critical examination of practice
Collaboration	Educators strategize root causes and intervene to meet goals and objectives

Figure 5.1 Broad assumptions of teacher efficacy

Lillejord and Børte have presented findings and assertions from a meta-analysis of 73 studies, to develop guidelines and recommendations for teacher evaluation. The authors have cited relevant research to address the foundational confusion that educators have been met with through policy, implementation and assumptions. Jones et al. (2019) also concluded that the two school reform efforts, collaborative teaching and teacher evaluation, are at odds with each other and that a collaborative form of evaluation should be researched and implemented.

The question remains as to why teacher evaluation is stuck between accountability and promoting teachers' professional learning. As we saw in Chapter 1, teacher evaluation rubrics in the United States are classroom-heavy. This is at odds with collaborative school reforms. Current rubrics emphasize and prioritize the behaviors, actions and strategies used in the moment, during the lesson, by the teacher to the students. The teacher's actions during the lesson are the focus of evaluation documents—the equivalent of watching a basketball player shoot a free throw and then making an overall judgement about their basketball playing ability. If basketball coaches operated like that, they would not win many games. We have reduced our profession to a set of narrowly defined skills. Policymakers have reduced the need for principals and teachers to act as professionals, at least in the context of teacher evaluations.

High-Stakes Evaluations

High-stakes evaluations have four characteristic traits (Lillejord & Børte, 2019). They are:

- Summative: the evaluation is in writing, documented and filed for a variety of purposes by the organization or manager.

- Promotional: the evaluation at some time, now or in the future, could be used to support promotional purposes.

- Compensational: the evaluation is used to determine an employee's ability to earn more money.

- Ranking: the evaluation formally or informally ranks employees in relation to one another.

If any one of these four factors exists in an evaluation, it is high stakes. This clearly applies to teacher evaluations. It's intentional: politicians who push for new evaluations tell us there should be consequences for teachers who don't meet standards.

But with high-stakes evaluations come unintended consequences that can have a negative effective on the culture of the school. First, deficiencies are put in writing. This has a profound effective on the self-efficacy of the teacher. There is an inordinate amount of pressure on teachers to ensure nothing negative shows up on an evaluation (Lillejord & Børte, 2019). That's true even if becoming aware of a weakness could create an opportunity to improve. Second, high-stakes evaluations pit self-interest against the desire to improve. Almost all teachers love their job. But who doesn't want to make more money? Linking evaluation to compensation makes teachers eager for positive evaluation regardless of accuracy. Third, the ranking of teachers creates competition amongst teachers, comparisons, jealousy or feelings of inadequacy. Under these pressure-packed circumstances, schools have found that it is extremely difficult to cultivate a professional environment where people are learning together.

The presence of high-stakes student assessment tied to these systems makes these consequences even worse—teachers are teaching to the test and to the teacher evaluation, not doing what their best professional judgement tells them will promote learning.

It's no surprise that teacher evaluation doesn't fulfill its goal of promoting professional growth—instead it's used as a disconnected quality assurance tool to fulfill human resource requirements, state law or collective bargaining arrangements. Only a few "deviant" schools have been able to navigate these requirements and create learning cultures where professional learning thrives and student achievement and growth skyrocket.

Those schools have somehow managed to use the tools in a manner that does not obstruct their formative desires.

 ## Teachers as Professionals

Part of the reason we do not see the desired results with teacher evaluation systems is that teachers are regarded as having a low professional status, and are even labeled semiprofessionals.

Lillejord & Børte have described professionals as:

- having an in-depth training and certification, and regulation from the group to ensure quality;

- having a common knowledge base from consulting research and experience, using discretion to renew and share new knowledge, developing standards for good practice;

- providing high-quality services, relevant to society and context;

- being organized collegially with autonomy and solving problems collectively.

Although not all professions consistently possess all these traits, an ability to set standards and procedures among themselves is central to professionals' work. "Ideally, wrongful assumptions are corrected, replaced with new evidence and insights, communicated among members of the profession, who adjust practice accordingly" (p. 5).

As Lillejord & Børte noted, one reason behind teachers' lack of professional status is that the procedures they follow are created by external governing bodies. At least part of their functioning is a result of outside forces seeking to control their actions, right down to the types of questions they ask of students, on a rubric, scored by someone else. In the United States, we discourage the practice of teaching and have reduced it to a set of skills and behaviors to be measured, rated and assessed out of the context of the actual work.

It is hard to exhibit all of the professional qualities when mandates from lawmakers and policymakers do not encourage professional behaviors. Educators may be semiprofessional, but only because the bureaucrats won't let them be professional.

Creating a Learning Evaluation

Creating an evaluation system that allows teachers to grow goes hand in hand with recognizing teacher professionalism. Lillejord & Borte (2019) have argued that an effective evaluation is oriented to process oriented and based in inquiry. Such a system would also allow teachers to generate knowledge for practice. It would be facilitated by school leaders, involve the cyclical critique and criticism of shared, documented knowledge and build upon past work to agree on good practice. These goals also describe professional learning communities. Such communities satisfy professionals' need to act creatively and innovate.

A teacher evaluation system designed to meet these goals would assess how teachers engage in formative and formal collective inquiry. It would have process-oriented objectives and goals—assessing how the work gets done first, and the results secondarily. Embedding formative practices into their culture, norms and process is far more impactful than observing teachers once a semester for a performance evaluation. By changing our teacher evaluation systems to support true professional learning environments, we can bridge the accountability versus learning gap.

A New Foundation

> While most schools believe in continuous improvement, they may not practice the process proven to produce results for students.
>
> (Killion and Roy, 2009)

The measurement of teacher effectiveness has proven difficult to define. The attempt to locate, identify, define and communicate the idiosyncrasies of teaching has produced a volume of isolated methods. None of those methods means anything or has any real impact on students out of context. We need a new foundation. The building blocks of this foundation are already known: collaboration, collective efficacy, collective inquiry and context.

Teachers should not be presented with a rubric, method or program except as a tool to use during collaboration. All potentially effective methods should be presented to teacher teams before they're implemented. Teachers need to discuss items with their team in the context of their school, classroom, subject, academic standard, goal and objective before a strategy is ever attempted in a classroom. To hand teachers a document with elements that they are expected to use, outside of context, creates generic teachers unable to implement strategies for the betterment of their students.

For example, most teacher evaluation rubrics have a section on checking for student understanding or questioning tactics. Randomly implementing a formative assessment or questioning scheme does nothing for student learning. What if the students don't really understand what is being explained, but don't want to say they didn't understand for fear they will be accused of not paying attention? Or what if some students didn't understand the lesson but don't know how to articulate their questions because the material was far too advanced for them? For that matter, what if a teacher doesn't follow the protocol of "checking for understanding" because they have established a classroom dynamic in which students speak up if they don't understand? Walking into a classroom to observe a teacher and looking for these items without background knowledge of the lesson is useless.

Act Now!

The supposed goals of teacher evaluation can be effectively realized through developing measures to evaluate collaborative teaching (Jones et al., 2019). Current teacher evaluation policies need to take a back seat to collaborative reforms.

Teacher evaluation systems should be overhauled immediately in order to:

- remove numerical ratings;
- blur effectiveness rankings to promote leadership and denounce categorizations of teachers;
- promote discussion;
- increase collaboration;
- influence collective efficacy;
- incentivize debate;
- build capacity through shared decision making and governance.

Case Study: The Evaluation Conversation

Have you heard this conversation before?

Principal: I am going to be using the district rubric again this year to evaluate you. When I come to your classroom, I will be looking for the elements in domain 2 of the rubric. Domain 2 focuses on your activities in the classroom teaching a lesson. It is 75% of your observational score.

Teacher: Will you give every element a rating in Domain 2 during one lesson, as you did last year?

Principal: Yes, the district requirement is that each item is scored during an observation.

Teacher: How is that possible? How can you come into a classroom for 45 minutes and see everything in Domain 2? There are 10 subdomains and 60 elements.

Principal: I will do my best. I will score each subdomain in Domain 2. If you disagree or have evidence of accomplishing an element of a subdomain that does not match my rating, please bring it to our conference. Will I see every element in Domain 2 during one lesson? Of course not. But hopefully, throughout the year, with multiple observations I will see everything.

Teacher: ...Okay.

This conversation represents a best-case scenario: a principal who wants to be fair and recognizes that the system requires them to do the impossible. But the teacher is still left worrying that they'll lose points because a single lesson didn't include every element of their teaching. The lesson they teach on evaluation day may even be less effective than normal because they struggle to include all 60 teaching elements.

It is Time to Start Over

> When educators engage in continuous learning, student learning is improved.
> (Donohoo, 2017, p. 51)

Teacher evaluation systems in this country do more harm than good to student learning because they focus on the outputs of effective teaching (teachers teaching lessons) instead of the inputs (teacher collaboration, lesson planning, data analysis and professional learning). We need to redesign our teacher evaluations systems to measure the behaviors and activities that increase collective efficacy—the number one factor in student achievement (Donohoo, Hattie & Eells, 2018).

New Assumptions

All evaluation programs are built on assumptions. We need new assumptions about effective teaching to guide the construction of teacher evaluations. And unlike the current, unexamined assumptions, the new assumptions need to be explicitly stated before a new system is built. A fundamental shift in belief, philosophy and operation must advance for adult professional learning and student achievement to increase.

New Assumption #1: Schools Are Not Businesses

Schools are their own, unique entities. We are not going to get anywhere by treating them like for-profit institutions.

Schools should be willing to try anything that will help students. If looking into other industries and using some of their strategies will help educators better serve students, then they should do so. But what we've done with regard to teacher evaluation isn't an example of that. Instead, we copied a flawed system from the corporate world. Modern teacher evaluations systems mirror three models used in business (Lavigne, 2014):

- Rating scales: measuring performance to a documented standard
- Ranking method: employees are ranked against each other in assessed performance
- Forced distribution: a bell curve is applied to teacher performance

All of these approaches are subject to systematic problems that have been documented in literature and respond to one another, each attempting to combat the flaws with the other methods.

> Corporate America has had its fair share of high-stakes evaluations and many of the most aggressive models have been scaled back. The failures and challenges faced in the business world's version of high-stakes evaluation paints an uncertain picture for the application of such models in education. The history of high stakes in previous educational efforts offers additional concerns.
>
> (Lavigne, 2014, p. 6)

Educators should consult research from other fields and collaborate with other professionals. But policymakers should not copy business models of operation blindly and think that they will have a positive impact on schools, especially if the action has not had a positive impact in other fields. It is time we come to the realization that schools are unique. There is no other societal institution that they compare to, because of our clients and their diverse needs.

New Assumption #2: Principals As Team Leaders Determine Effectiveness

Principals facilitate and lead teacher teams as the most effective way to assess teacher effectiveness. Principals and teachers who work together effectively have a greater impact on student achievement (Owen, 2015). Through observations, interactions, conversations and the real work of engaging in school teams, the principal will make determinations of a teacher's effectiveness within the context and culture of the local school.

This system is very different from a set of standardized skills, domains, behaviors or classroom observations alone. The school teams create the environment where collective efficacy can thrive, and a teacher's ability to function within a collaborative culture becomes the primary subject being evaluated. Each team, guided by the principal, provides multiple views and perspectives on high-quality teaching, creating a shared meaning and understanding, reducing bias and placing emphasis on what actually works.

This new assumption would add context to the classroom and the school, linking teachers and principals to the shared mission of the school and to collaborative action plans to move forward. It would also reduce bias, because the meaning of quality teaching is constructed collectively and shared.

New Assumption #3: Success Isn't Individual

Teachers demonstrate their effectiveness by being an active member of a professional learning community. The number one factor in student achievement is collective efficacy (Donohoo, Hattie & Eells, 2018), so the collective is what we need to build up.

This new assumption assesses a teacher's ability to perform in a professional learning community, and his or her contributions to the collective efficacy of the team. While completely eliminating subjectivity from a performance evaluation is impossible, aligning evaluation systems to this new assumption will free principals from evaluating the outputs of teaching (delivering lessons) and instead put principals on the front end, working with teachers on inputs: lesson planning, data analysis, professional learning, resource sharing and collaboration. The best way for a teacher to demonstrate their effectiveness is to be a part of a vibrant and productive learning community. Technical teaching, engaging students, delivering content, pedagogy, presentation—that's all the result of collaboration.

New Assumption #4: General > Specific

Teacher evaluation rubrics are a tool to guide teams through processes of inquiry. They should be broad and customizable to local schools, anchored in collaborative processes, focusing on the few things that matter most to increase adult professional learning and student achievement: collaboration, data analysis, goal setting, problem solving and progress monitoring. In essence, a professional learning community.

Future rubrics should be living documents that shift and change as the needs of the teachers and students shift and change. In those documents, the terms and concepts used should be broad and possibly have multiple meanings, based on the context of the local school and areas of development for individual teachers and teams. Open-ended documents will allow principals to focus on the inputs of effective teaching in order to have greater influence on the outputs.

With a de-emphasis of endless specialized skills will come a welcome shortening of evaluation documents. Teachers do not need pages upon pages of bullet points emphasizing effective teaching that may or may not be relevant to their needs or needs of their students. Instead, the documents should be tools that incorporate elements of a professional learning community, emphasizing trends in current research, guiding teachers, teams and the administration through processes of collective inquiry.

New Assumption #5: Communicate, Communicate, Communicate

Today's evaluations assume a teacher's communication to students in front of the class is the only thing that matters. This new assumption values conversations, discussions and interactions among teachers and between teachers and principals. New evaluation models will encourage the creation of systematic standard operating procedures around these conversations. The new documents will serve as a guide and communication tool to set goals, discuss programing, assess, implement and change. Teachers and principals discuss what is working and what is not working. In the process, any documentation teachers or principals needed to have will be there ready for review.

The most cutting-edge research tells us that "Collective efficacy is increased through collaborative learning structures" (Donahoo, 2017, p. 54). Using evaluation documents to communicate, not just document, will provide a structured way to ensure that teachers are asking the right questions, collectively solving problems, building cohesion, learning about and from one another, setting goals, spreading their influence and creating learning environments and tasks that meet student needs.

Teacher Evaluation Assumptions Comparison

The new assumptions for evaluating teachers are different from the current assumptions in philosophy, implementation and operation. Below is a chart comparing the faulty assumptions from chapter 3 and the new impactful assumptions of teacher evaluation.

Professional Learning Communities Defined

What's needed is a teacher evaluation system linked to proven systems of teacher inquiry, collaboration and program implementation. Professional learning communities (PLCs) provide the blueprint for just such a system.

A PLC, as defined by DuFour, DuFour, Eake, and Many (2006), is a group of educators "committed to working collaboratively in ongoing processes of collective inquiry and action research to achieve better results for the students they serve" (p. 14). The central idea of a learning community is that student learning will improve only when teachers have the opportunity for job-embedded professional development on a regular basis.

A PLC has some basic characteristics, the first being a shared mission, vision and goals, all of which are focused on student learning. For a PLC to be successful, all stakeholders must embrace high expectations and make a commitment to the learning of each student. This goal reinforces the moral purpose and collective responsibility that make the day-to-day work of teachers so important (DuFour et al., 2006).

The second characteristic of a learning community is a collaborative culture with a focus on student learning. A PLC is ideally composed of grade-level or subject-matter teams that meet regularly to achieve common goals. Team members are responsible for creating common assessments,

Assumption Comparison

Teacher Evaluation Assumptions	
Faulty Assumptions	**Impactful Assumptions**
Education should mimic the business world.	School are unique entities. Best practices from other domains are consulted, but not blindly adopted.
Principals observing teachers is the most effective way to determine teacher effectiveness.	Principals facilitate and lead teacher teams as the most effective way to assess teacher effectiveness.
Working in isolation, alone with students in the classroom, is the most effective way for teachers to demonstrate their effectiveness.	Teachers demonstrate their effectiveness by being active members of a Professional Learning Community.
Teacher evaluation rubrics must incorporate as many characteristics of effective teaching as possible.	Teacher evaluation rubrics focus on processes of collective inquiry, collaboration, context.
Teacher must employ a cadre of "research-based" instructional strategies in the classroom, during a lesson, to demonstrate their effectiveness.	Teachers work within collaborative teams to assess their needs as professionals and the needs of their students, in order to collectively research, prioritize, select and implement strategies to improve professional learning and student learning, demonstrating their effectiveness.
Document, Document, Document	Communicate, Communicate, Communicate

Figure 5.2 Assumptions comparison

analyzing results and planning for differences in student learning. These actions help keep team members accountable to one another and create a systematic process for collaboration.

The third essential element of the PLC model is collective inquiry into best practices and current performance. Educators must be able to take a candid look at their current practices and student performance. They must then work together to discover best practices for their situation. In a successful learning community, educators should be oriented to action. Learning by doing is essential to a PLC because change will not occur until teachers act. Teachers must also be committed to continuous improvement. They should strive to gather evidence of current learning, develop new strategies and analyze their impact.

Abundant evidence exists that PLCs are highly effective. Education researcher Michael Schmoker (2006) has spoken of their importance when he stated that "the use of professional learning communities is the best, least expensive, most professionally rewarding way to improve schools... Such communities hold immense, unprecedented hope for schools and the improvement of teaching" (p. 106). Numerous studies back this up to support the effectiveness of PLCs. One study conducted by Louis and Marks (1998) found that when a school uses adult learning concepts, teachers set higher expectations, students receive more support in achieving learning goals, classroom pedagogy is of considerably higher quality and achievement levels are higher (DuFour et al., 2006). DuFour et al. (2004) focused their research on collaboration, communication, data-driven analysis, collective intelligence and collective response to student learning, school-wide systems and school culture.

The title of Roland S. Barth's book *Improving Schools from Within* (1991) suggests the reason that PLCs are so effective in improving performance. External mandates from groups or individuals outside the school community and culture will not have a lasting effect. The improvement of schools must come from members of the school community. "A key to improving schools from within, then, lies in improving the interactions among teachers and between teachers and principals" (Barth, 1991, p. 28).

From a principal and teacher perspective, a Learning Evaluation system reduces bias. Teachers and administrators are consistently involved in collaborations and conversations, considering the best methods for teams to employ in order to increase student achievement. The common language of the school is created by the professional educators, not handed down to them from somewhere else. Instead of teachers being rated based on their effectiveness in a domain by one person (principal) through an observation, based on a standardized rubric, the common language of school teams—established in the school, amongst the staff and employed through collaborative systems—becomes the driver for evaluations. The evaluation tool should guide the entire teaching staff through collective process to collaborate, set goals, plan instruction, analyze student data, seek improvement and help others improve. A Learning Evaluation system gives the principal the freedom to participate in all of the school's teams, thus truly serving as an instructional leader and school improvement partner. Such a system will increase employee engagement and increase organizational commitment.

Teachers who work effectively within their teams fail, grow and learn. Consequently, they become better teachers. Principals will also become more effective evaluators. Through observations, interactions, conversations and the real work of engaging in school teams, the principal will make determinations of a teacher's effectiveness within the context and culture of the local school, as opposed to by reference to a set of standardized skills, domains, behaviors or classroom observations alone, based on a rubric. The school teams become the vehicle for teacher efficacy, and a teacher's ability to function within a professional team becomes the primary focus of evaluation.

Directly connected to employee engagement is organizational commitment. Organizational commitment refers to the psychological bond that ties an employee to the organization (Nehmeh, 2009). The stronger the bond, the more likely it is that organizational initiatives will be successful. By involving teachers in the evaluation via a collective process, schools make it likely that their organizational commitment will increase. A Learning Evaluation system has the potential to increase a teacher's involvement in his or her individual school. Any increase in organizational commitment would garner increases in leadership capacity, teacher per-formance and student learning.

A Learning Evaluation system can also benefit a school's principal and assistant principal. A building administrator spends an inordinate amount of time evaluating teacher classroom performance. Even a "small" building can house many teachers, each requiring multiple observations and thus evaluations. Using a Learning Evaluation system allows the building administrators to focus on more strategic issues, including curriculum integration, assessment, pedagogy, professional learning, cultural awareness and proficiency and student- and family-related issues.

In general, workers are more receptive to receiving constructive criticism from peers rather than a supervisor. Because each teacher is a practitioner, any constructive feedback relates directly to the practice of teaching, and teachers know that it is coming from someone who performs the same duties as they do. In a Learning Evaluation, teachers both provide and receive feedback from their colleagues, becoming authentic instructional leaders. The work environment becomes a laboratory of continuous improvement in which each teacher plays the role of scientist, participant and instructional leader.

Learning Evaluation systems will provide a more consistent, customizable evaluation for teachers. Rather than looking for strengths or weaknesses of each teacher based on a predetermined rubric, the principal will look for teacher contributions to the school teams and assess their capacity to improve in a learning environment. A Learning Evaluation system will thus allow evaluations to be customizable and open-ended. The school teams can identify the strengths and weaknesses of each other, set goals for improvement of practice and adapt the evaluation to meet their needs.

Charlotte Danielson stated that nurturing great teaching has become a difficult task to complete in policy and practice (Danielson, 2016). Danielson elaborated, for *Education Week*, "I'm deeply troubled by the transformation of teaching from a complex profession requiring nuanced judgement to the performance of certain behaviors that can be ticked off on a checklist" (Danielson, 2016, n.p.). Danielson then went on to explain several points of emphasis for future evaluation conversations, one of which, she concluded, should involve evaluation systems that encourage professional learning, inquiry and trust.

The traditional, individualistic, observational evaluations currently in use have run their course. It is time educational leaders start demanding of policymakers that the work educators engage in to increase student achievement becomes what is evaluated, leveraging the power of instructional leadership and increasing student achievement.

There is a better way to evaluate teachers. We have already learned from recent reform failures that the current system is not producing the desired results, and teachers and principals are increasingly frustrated. We already know how to improve schools: professional learning communities, which are the most rewarding and successful professional initiative for teachers and principals. By shifting our thinking from observing individual teachers to assessing a teacher's ability to perform within a professional learning community, we sweep away the old and make room for a new foundation.

Tips and Talking Points

The Four Cs of Creating a Learning Evaluation System

The four Cs of creating a teacher evaluation system are *collective inquiry, collaboration, collective efficacy* and *context.*

Collective inquiry refers to a teaching team's ability to look at an educational issue from a variety of perspectives and construct a shared meaning of the problem and all possible solutions, based on the various perspectives. The second step is to prioritize the problems, seek out solutions and prioritize a short list of actionable steps based on the culture, resources available and the ability of the team.

Collaboration refers to a teaching team's ability to identify a problem, agree on action steps, administer those action steps, assess impact, identify new possible actions steps, administer the new actions step cyclically, and eventually solve the problem.

Collective efficacy is the team's ability to inquire about educational issues and collaborate to solve the problem in an effective way collectively. Collective efficacy culminates with team success and results from collaboration.

Context is what lies in the background of the three other Cs. The context of the local school, their needs, wants, goals, aspirations, students and staff needs, is what brings an evaluation from something out there done to educators to something they do together.

Which brings us back to the PLC model. PLCs are oriented toward results. Without results, we are not collaborating. But we cannot not trust standardized portrayals of "results." Results for a teacher should mean learning—their own and that of fellow teachers and students.

Learning about yourself as a teacher, learning about your students, as learners, and as people. Using what you learn about yourself and students to promote their well-being—those are results.

This may be a shortcoming of the PLC models as presented in the literature. PLCs are results-oriented, but what results? Scores, graduation rates, disproportionality, reading levels, growth models? We have become too narrow in what we mean by results. Teachers simply need to learn about their students as people first, and then learners. If they know about them in this way, they will be able to work within their collaborative teaching teams to devise the best plan possible to help students grow academically, behaviorally and socially.

The most effective way to increase student achievement is for teachers to inquire collectively and collaborate. Results need to be defined within the context of process-oriented goals and objectives. The new results of PLCs are admittedly subjective in nature, defined in the local context of the school and verified by longitudinal normative data. But that's a good thing. We should stop attempting quick fixes in education. We know too much about how change occurs in a school—indeed must happen in schools—and the types of foundational cultures that must be built to encourage the desired change.

If we can bring the four Cs on board as the foundation of our teacher evaluation systems, we can build a system that encourages and assesses the things that we already know have a tremendous impact on student learning. That is the goal of this work. As you will see in the coming chapters, a teacher evaluation system can be built to assess the few things that teachers and principals do to increase student learning and achievement.

The Four Cs of a Learning Evaluation

Collective Inquiry

Teachers...
• Inquire together
• Ask questions
• Answer questions, read
• Conduct action research
• Review data
• Discuss perceptions
• Observe and reflect on their practices
• Are knowledgeable about their work and the work of their peers.
• Have influence over the questions they explore and methods used to solve problems.

Collaboration

Teachers gather information about...
• Themselves
• Team
• School
• Students
• Parents

Teachers use that information to...
• Solve problems
• Increase adult professional learning
• Increase student achievement
• Influence well-being

Teachers collaborate to...
• Complete formal and informal needs assessments
• Strategize
• Prioritize
• Implement adult and student interventions
• Share governance of direction
• Create consensus to solve problems leading to cohesion
• Have influence over the strategies employed.

Collective Efficacy

Collaboration leads to collective efficacy. Teams, working together to solve problems, increases the efficacy of the professional staff.

Teachers find success as an organization, not simply as individuals.

Educators are interdependently linked to the success of the organization.

Through effective participation in processes of inquiry, teachers work together as a team to develop objectives and meet goals.

Context

The work of becoming a learning organization is having a productive working knowledge of context.

The context of the local school is an assumed piece of collective knowledge.

Educators that have a working knowledge of the context in which they work...
• Ask better questions
• Search for answers from schools similar to theirs
• Use local data to track progress
• Collaborate to implement, adapt, change and try initiatives, interventions and strategies

Figure 5.3 The four Cs of a Learning Evaluation

References

Barth, R. S. (1991). *Improving schools from within: Teachers, parents, and principals can make the difference*. San Francisco, CA: Jossey-Bass.

Danielson, C. (2016, April 20). Charlotte Danielson on rethinking teacher evaluation. *Education Week*. Retrieved from www.edweek.org/ew/articles/2016/04/20/charlotte-danielson-on-rethinking-teacher-evaluation.html.

Donohoo, J., Hattie, J., & Eells, R. (2018, March). The power of collective efficacy. *Educational Leadership, 75*(6), 40–44.

Donohoo, J. (2017). Collective efficacy: How educators' beliefs impact student learning. Thousand Oaks, CA: Corwin.

Dufour, R., DuFour, R., Eaker, R., & Many, T. (2006). *Learning by doing: A handbook for professional learning communities at work*. Alexandria, VA: Solution Tree.

DuFour, R., Eaker, R., Karhanek, G., & Dufour, R. (2004). Whatever it takes: How professional learning communities respond when kids don't learn. Alexandria, VA: Solution Tree.

Jones, N. D., Bettini, E., & Brownell, M. (2019). Competing strands of educational reform policy: Can collaborative school reform and teacher evaluation reform be reconciled? *The Elementary School Journal, 119*(3), 468–486.

Killion, J., & Roy, P. (2009). *Becoming a learning school*. Oxford, OH: National Staff Development Council.

Lavigne, A. L. (2014). Exploring the intended and unintended consequences of high-stakes teacher evaluation on schools, teachers, and students. *Teachers College Record, 116*(1).

Louis, K.S., & Marks, H. M. (1998). Does professional learning community affect the classroom? Teachers' work and student experiences in restructuring schools. *American Journal of Education, 106*(4), 532–575.

Lillejord, S., & Børte, K. (2019). Trapped between accountability and professional learning? School leaders and teacher evaluation. *Professional Development in Education, 46*(2), 274–291.

Nehmeh, R. (2009). What is organizational commitment, why should managers want it in their workforce and is there any cost-effective way to secure it? Zug, Switzerland: Swiss Management Center University.

Owen, S.M. (2015). Teacher professional learning communities in innovative contexts. *Professional Development in Education*, *41*(1), 57–74. doi:10.1080/19415257.2013.869504.

Saunders, W. M., Goldenberg, C. N., & Gallimore, R. (2009). Increasing achievement by focusing grade-level teams on improving classroom learning: A prospective, quasi-experimental study of Title I schools. *American Educational Research Journal*, *46*(4), 1006–1033.

Schmoker, M. (2006). *Results now: How we can achieve unprecedented improvements in teaching and learning* (1st ed.). Alexandria, VA: Association for Supervision & Curriculum Development.

Learning Evaluation System

6

Theory of Action: A Learning Evaluation

> The best way to eliminate the disparity between what we say and what we do and to invite the jugular questions is to forge a unified theory of action, shared across a school or district, that both explains and determines the actions that members take as individuals and as a community.
>
> (Moss and Brokehart, 2012, p. 9)

Consulting research on performance appraisals, current teacher appraisal policies and programs and systems, and the research on learning organizations and professional learning communities (PLCs), we can now set out a theory of action. Teachers are assessed on their ability to perform in a PLC. As a result, teacher reflection increases. Teachers become more aware of the impact of their actions. Professional learning and status advances, becoming more relevant and applicable to their jobs. As a result, student learning increases.

In previous chapters, we have laid the foundation for a new process. Traditional systems and structures have not served our teachers or children, but only as a result of the faulty assumptions on which the system was built. Those assumptions have compounded into a system that is incoherent, inconsistent, focused on the wrong actions and *lacks processes to positively impact professional learning, teacher improvement and school improvement.* The literature is consistent on that point. For whatever the reason, teacher evaluation has not worked. Now that we have new

Theory of Action

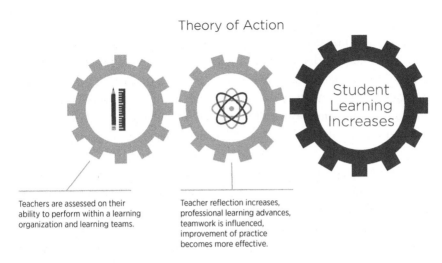

Teachers are assessed on their ability to perform within a learning organization and learning teams.

Teacher reflection increases, professional learning advances, teamwork is influenced, improvement of practice becomes more effective.

Figure 6.1 Theory of action

assumptions a system can be built with the correct processes and with appropriate emphasis on teacher and principal actions that have an impact on student learning.

Dangerous Aspirations

A new evaluation is presented in this chapter. True to the term "evaluation," it is subjective in nature and requires principals and teachers to embrace a standard of professionalism not previously realized. A *Teacher Evaluation Rubric, Student-Centered Evaluation Rubric and Assumptions Guide* and a *Learning Script* are provided to start schools on a path to build an evaluation that will work for them.

I am reluctant to release these documents. My fear is that they will be misused, in the same manner that the term "PLC" has been misused by so many. I must stress that these are simply examples of a process-oriented evaluation system based on PLC principles. The danger in all of this lies with people who think they can print these documents and use them tomorrow. There is a lot of frontloading that has to happen before the documents can be used. We are attempting to make a big shift in school cultures. We are one hundred years into this mess. There is no quick fix.

These documents, and any other document that educators use to improve their practice, need to be introduced, examined, placed into a local context and collectively implemented, reduced or expanded. A learning evaluation will make teachers' and principals' lives easier by focusing their attention on what matters most. However, if the faulty structures and assumptions of the old system are not critically examined first and rebuilt, there is danger in moving too fast in finally creating a system that works.

The important aspect about the documents is not the literal words, or even the documents themselves, but the mindframe from which they were created. It is my hope that if reading this book has inspired anyone with the power to create a teacher evaluating system, they would consult these documents as examples only, and use the processes to create a local system that works for their district or school.

High-quality teachers have an impact on student performance and collaborate with each other to do so. If a school desires to improve student performance, the most effective action educators can take is to increase collective efficacy (Donohoo, Hattie & Eells, 2018). Therefore, I am advocating for a teacher evaluation system that evaluates teachers' ability to contribute to a learning organization, in place of an observational teacher evaluation (measurement) system. The current mechanism for evaluating teachers is limiting educational professionals' ability to leverage the power of teachers to work together in the school improvement process. Donohoo, Hattie and Eells (2018) released an updated list of the practices that have the most profound effect on student learning. The report found that the most impactful construct that teachers can engage to increase student learning is collective efficacy.

> As it becomes more apparent that teaching is a complex technology exercised in rather fluid classroom contexts, it likewise becomes apparent that teachers should have the autonomy and authority to decide what is best to do in any given circumstance, rather than having to respond to bureaucratic policies and rules that assign a decontextualized uniformity and simplicity to teaching and learning.
>
> (Sergiovanni and Starratt, 2007, p. 359)

Bringing it All Together

The well-documented problems with performance evaluations and teacher evaluations require us to change. The case against measuring teacher effectiveness is strong. We need to move toward a learning evaluation that is broad and uniform enough to bridge the formative and summative gap. We need an evaluation that embraces the principles and processes of collective inquiry and collaboration: a system that is unapologetically subjective, and that seeks to solve problems in the local context and needs of students and teachers. By focusing on the broad processes needed to move any school forward, the document can serve as a foundation for any school thinking to implement a learning evaluation.

 # "Emphasize This, Not That"

New teacher evaluations will have to change in order to cultivate the desired results of adult and student learning. Below is a chart comparing traditional teacher evaluations with a new emphasis on a learning evaluation.

Teacher Evaluation Emphasis Comparison	
Emphasize this...	Not That...
Elements of a learning organization	Business or corporate performance models
Principal facilitation of teacher teams	Observe teachers individually
Broad-based rubrics highlighting collaborative processes to plan and implement agreed upon methods	Assessment of individuals conducting isolated techniques, programs, strategies, models...
Communication, conversation, debate	Documentation, scripting lessons, rating scales
Process-oriented goals	Goals of student achievement out of context
Learning progressions	Categories of effectiveness

Figure 6.2 Teacher evaluation emphasis comparison

 # Learning Evaluation Rubric

The Learning Evaluation Rubric is a broad, fluid document that schools can use to create a teacher evaluation system to meet their needs. It is by its nature subjective. The subjectivity of the system allows schools and districts the freedom to create shared meaning, reducing bias, increasing buy-in and promoting a shared understanding of the local schools' goals and objectives. Without teacher influence and the ability of teachers and principals to share ideas and decision-making, teacher effectiveness will not advance. Building a system upon the correct assumptions will require teachers and principals that are willing to let go of the old ways and embrace new ways. The traditional, observation-based teacher evaluation systems have done more harm than good to the profession. By changing our ways and embracing the collective efforts we know work, we can remove the largest barrier to teacher and school improvement: individualized, isolated evaluations.

Learning Evaluation Assumptions

The Learning Evaluation Rubric is conceptualized in terms of collective and collaborative principles. The norms that should be established are

- Student learning-focused mission
- Contributions to collaborative teams
- Data utilization
- Goal setting
- Curriculum and pedagogy
- Improvement of practice
- Observation, examination, adaptation of practices

Learning Evaluation Assumptions
The learning evaluation assumptions are action-oriented for teachers and principals.
Educational professionals view themselves as learners
Respectful, honest communication is the norm
Solving problems is a team-oriented task
Educational professionals are strategically placed in teams for purposeful, deliberate, intentional, data-driven collaboration and problem solving
Educational administrators set up the processes, systems and procedures for professional teams to meet and collaborate
Educational Administrators facilitate the direction of the school and teams, setting goals, outcomes, action plans and fidelity to the process, and acting as a thinking partner for teachers.

Figure 6.3 Learning Evaluation assumptions

Learning Evaluation Rubric

Indicators	Evidence Observed			
Indicators	**Impactful Contributor**	**Learning to Contribute**	**Inconsistent Contributor**	**Non-Contributor**
Student Learning Focused Mission	The teacher embraces and believes that the mission of the school is to ensure that all students learn at high levels.			The teacher does not embrace and believe that the mission of the school is to ensure that all students learn at high levels.
Contributions to Collaborative School Teams	Teacher contributes to teams by sharing resources, ideas, strategies, data and best practices through processes of collective inquiry. The teacher consistently works within teams to increase their own effectiveness and the effectiveness of other professional educators, influencing adult professional learning and student achievement positively.	Teacher is learning to contribute to teams by sharing resources, ideas, strategies and best practices. Teacher benefits professionally from engaging in teams that have an impact on student achievement. Teacher is learning to contribute to the professional growth of their peers.	Teacher does not consistently contribute to teams, influencing inconsistent professional growth for themselves and/or others. Student achievement may be negatively impacted by the teacher's inconsistent participation in school teams and processes of collective inquiry.	Teacher does not contribute to school teams or processes of collective inquiry and does not take responsibility for student learning, resulting in a negative impact on collective efficacy and student achievement.
Data Utilization	Teacher consistently uses data to address problems collectively, intentionally and strategically. Teacher uses data to examine and interpret individual and collective pedagogical impact on student achievement. Teacher works within teams to identify students who need additional support, students who need enrichment and to identify instructional strategies that increase student learning and achievement.	Teacher is learning to use data consistently, influencing identified pedagogical areas of improvement. Teacher is learning to use data in a more precise manner in order to influence their own and their team's professional learning and student needs.	Lack of consistency in data utilization has a neutral or negative effect on improving identified instructional weaknesses individually and collectively, as well as student identification for support or enrichment.	Teacher does not use data to improve pedagogical practices and identify student needs.
Goal Setting	Teacher consistently establishes class/subject and individual goals of student achievement. Teacher develops action plans in collaboration with their team to meet those goals. Teacher works with their team to develop goals of professional learning based on the needs of the students according to data.	Teacher is learning to establish class/subject and/or individual goals of student achievement based on the needs of his/her students. Teacher is learning to understand a clear link between adult professional learning goals and student achievement.	Teacher does not consistently establish class/subject and/or individual goals of student achievement. Teacher does not understand the link between professional learning, goal setting and student achievement.	Teacher does not establish class/subject goals of student achievement. Teacher does not facilitate individual goals of student achievement or action plans. Teacher does not understand the role of professional learning in raising student achievement and improving professionally.

Figure 6.4 Learning Evaluation 1

Learning Evaluation Rubric

Indicators	Evidence Observed			
Indicators	**Impactful Contributor**	**Learning to Contribute**	**Inconsistent Contributor**	**Non-Contributor**
Curriculum and Pedagogy	Teacher consistently works in collaborative teams to establish a guaranteed and viable curriculum for content areas and subjects; clarify essential learning, creating pacing guidelines, implementing summative, formative and imbedded assessments, and collaborates to try new and research-based instructional strategies with team members.	Teacher is learning to implement agreed-upon curriculum and pedagogical practices. Teacher is learning to use assessments to influence professional practices consistently.	Inconsistent adherence to curriculum and pedagogical practices is detrimental to the alignment of instructional and assessment practices, affecting anticipated professional growth and student learning.	Teacher does not contribute to the work of collaborative teams to establish a guaranteed and viable curriculum for content areas and subjects. Lack of contribution inhibits the discussion of new and research-based instructional strategies with team members.
Improvement of Practice	Teacher consistently works within teams to maximize their own strengths, and improve on their own weaknesses. Teacher works within teams to assist in maximizing other team members' strengths and assist in helping them improve upon weaknesses.	Teacher is learning to work within teams to maximize their own strengths, improve on their own weaknesses. Teacher works within teams to assist in maximizing other team member's strengths and assist in helping them improve upon weaknesses.	Teacher does not consistently work within PLCs to maximize strengths and/or improve upon weaknesses. Sporadic participation with teams limits improvement of practice collectively.	Teacher does not use his/her strengths to improve student learning or reflect on and improve upon weaknesses. Teacher does not understand how to work within PLCs contributing to the improvement of others or oneself.
Examination of Practices	Teacher consistently works within collaborative teams to: • Observe, examine and adapt practice • Assess advancement of goals (student and adult) • Reflect on results • Determine next steps	Teacher is learning to consistently work within collaborative teams to: • Observe, examine and adapt practice • Assess advancement of goals • Reflect on results • Determine next steps	Teacher inconsistently engages effectively in processes of collective inquiry, learning individually and as a team. Professional growth and student achievement does not increase as a result.	Teacher is unable to • Observe, examine and adapt practice • Assess advancement of goals • Reflect on results • Determine next steps

Figure 6.5 Learning Evaluation 2

These norms are processes, not concepts, actions, meetings or strategies. They are processes to develop and choose strategies, programs, techniques, interventions and curriculums. Teachers are evaluated on their ability to engage in these processes and learn. These processes have their own underlying assumptions. It is the role of responsive leadership to ingrain these assumptions into the culture of the school.

Student Learning-Focused Mission

The mission and vision of the school is centered on student learning. This may seem simple in theory but seems to be harder in practice. By establishing this process and the underlying assumptions, a staff is on its way to becoming collectively effective. There are no excuses for students not learning or growing. The teachers either believe that they can have an impact on student achievement, or they don't. There is no middle ground, sliding scale or progressive rubric for this process. It starts with individual and collective belief that the teacher and the school can get the job done.

Teachers demonstrate that they are committed to student learning through the way they interact in their teams. By utilizing an evaluation that assesses the collaborative process, teams and teachers will become more committed, and the small percentage who aren't will be seen by the entire staff. Those individuals will then need to make a decision about their choice of a profession and can be dealt with individually through due process standards, policies, laws and procedures. A staff demonstrates a high level of commitment by contributing its efforts to the success of the organization, school, team, grade level, department. That in its essence is demonstrating your collective efficacy. It is assumed that teachers practice their work with a student learning-focused action and mindset.

Case Study: It All Starts With Belief

Mr. Casper was the new principal at Creekside Middle School. He had been asked to take the position by the assistant superintendent. Creekside had struggled to maintain minimum proficiency levels on state assessments, as well as local assessments, for the last five years. Mr. Casper learned very soon that the teachers at Creekside did not believe that they could have a positive impact on student learning. Mr. Casper knew that the first step at improving the school was to get the staff to believe. He spent the first year watching and learning about the teachers, finding and celebrating pockets of success by teachers, teacher teams and students. He celebrated those pockets of success with his staff and slowly turned the tide of the collective belief system.

Mr. Casper had a writing teacher, Mrs. Johnson, who was great. Every year she would introduce a writing procedure that engaged the kids in authentic literacy. Mrs. Johnson was also well respected by her peers. Mr. Casper quickly took notice and facilitated the process for Mrs. Johnson to teach the other members of the language arts team her processes. The other teachers were attentive: they had seen Mrs. Johnson's success over the years. Within a few months every language arts teacher in the building had the same protocol for engaging students in authentic writing. Mr. Casper jumped on that success and made it a point of emphasis, not just for teaching language arts, but for the teamwork displayed and the belief that they could be successful with all students.

Mr. Casper knew that before the school could engage in any processes to improve, it first needed to believe. After the staff began believing in its ability to influence student learning, then and only then could he facilitate the improvement of the professional staff and school as a whole.

Contributions to Collaborative Teams

Teacher collaboration has been linked extensively to student learning, growth and achievement. We know that when teachers work together, with a common goal and purpose, the collective experience, knowledge, wisdom and effectiveness increases and makes the entire school better.

Practices where teachers lead professional learning and learn from peers in collaborative support structures build school capacity. Student success is not bestowed upon the individual teacher; rather, teachers working together during the day, weeks and quarters of a school year hold ongoing professional conversations to improve their practice and meet their students' needs. Student achievement is influenced by teachers' collaborative endeavors (Goddard et al., 2015). As with all evaluation concepts, a learning evaluation also has foundational assumptions. In a learning evaluation, collaboration is an assumption of effective teaching. In fact, it might be the most important assumption having influence over the other domains. People that don't know how to collaborate, don't know how to collective analyze data, provide feedback to others....and the list goes on. This domain is the foundation of the school's efforts. Teacher collaboration assumes certain behaviors, traits, philosophies and values.

 ## Collaborative Teams Assumptions

Teachers in a Learning Evaluation assume certain aspects of collaboration. They:

- value input from one another;
- collectively solve problems;
- support one another;
- influence professional learning;
- share decision making;
- find, use and share resources;
- cultivate ideas, creativity and innovation.

Case Study: Teamwork

Third graders at Hamilton Hill Elementary had not performed well in recent years on the school's internal formative assessments or the state standardized reading assessment. Mrs. Pung, the principal, was a student learning expert and knew she had reading teaching experts on staff. She knew that through the right collaborative process, encouraging positive contributions from everyone, they could better prepare students in all grades to become proficient readers.

    Mrs. Pung met with her third-grade team leader, Mrs. Good. She started the conversation by asking Mrs. Good what she thought her team needed to show growth and an increase in student learning on their local formative assessments. Mrs. Good listed several items that would help them immediately. Mrs. Pung then asked Mrs. Good, "What do students coming to third grade not know that will help them prepare to become proficient readers?" Mrs. Good, a reading teaching expert in her own right, was able to list several skills and content areas that students might have missed in earlier grades, going back to Kindergarten. Mrs. Good was using her years of experience to draw back the items she had to emphasize every year for students who were reading below grade level.

Mrs. Pung then went to her other grade-level team leaders. They had the same conversation. By the time Mrs. Pung was done meeting with team leaders she had developed a concrete understanding of where the learning gaps were at each grade level. She brought the team leaders together for a collaboration. She presented to them her findings from her team leader meetings. The teachers were blown away. They have never looked at reading in a longitudinal way. At that point the team was able to have deep conversations about teaching reading, student learning, scope and sequence. The team was charged with taking the information presented to them and their thoughts back to their team to prioritize. The team came up with several ideas to be discussed by grade-level teams.

The grade-level teams met for collaboration. They discussed school-wide data, grade-level data and classroom-specific data. Based on the students' data for the current year and past trend data, the teams each provided a list of concepts to explore for professional learning, a list of skills to teach (now seeking to fill learning gaps), and a prioritized list of curriculum items that needed to be addressed before students left their grade at the end of the year. The team leaders presented their findings to Mrs. Pung. They had a plan!

Mrs. Pung was able to use the broad concept of collaboration to facilitate a plan of action to better serve students. Now imagine if their time was spent analyzing a rubric that emphasized what type of questions they asked students, or the students asked. Imagine Mrs. Pung using her time to observe each teacher individually and provide feedback. The problems they were facing would never have had a chance to be solved, because—like most problems in a school—they were not isolated issues but required a team effort.

Fast forward to the end of the year and I would imagine that Mrs. Pung's team leaders would be viewed as impactful contributors to collaborative teams. I would imagine that a few teachers that were not designated "team leaders" would have become so as well, and that most teachers would be viewed as contributors. There is no numerical score attached to the teacher's evaluation, there is no pay increase for being an impactful contributor as opposed to a contributor. Mrs. Pung subjectively categorizes teachers based on her interactions and observations of the teacher's ability to collaborate.

There was a case of non-contribution. Mrs. Pung had a second-grade teacher that refused to engage in the plan that her grade-level team and school team developed to improve reading achievement and growth. This teacher continually had negative things to say in meetings, was not following the agreed-upon plan and tried to "do her own thing"—but not in a creative way. She just wanted to do what she had always done.

Mrs. Pung should start a conversation with that teacher and highlight in the rubric and assumption guide where she thinks the teacher could improve. People need time to reflect and realize their own need for change. Mrs. Pung could highlight comments the teacher has made, items that she refused to engage in and her ability to work with her teams. Mrs. Pung would take those items, place them beside the rubric and assumption guide and attempt to show the teacher how to improve. Mrs. Pung should give the teacher time to improve and set up another meeting at a later date. If the teacher is unable to improve it would be noted in her evaluation and it would then become a human resources issue, because the teacher is a non-contributor. The key point here is that we are not going to make the good teachers jump through a bunch of hoops and complete a bunch of documents, when in reality the teachers that need to find another profession are a small percentage. The teachers that are not willing to be a part of a team enter a different process, to ensure that the legalities of removing them from the classroom are followed.

Data Utilization

Standardized testing has created an environment where diverse sources of data are not appreciated. "Multiple measures of assessment" is a term that has been represented in the assessment literature. The standardized assessments students are subjected to and high-stakes teacher evaluations have made our data utilization too constricted. The NCLB act incentivized schools to prioritize data utilization to show student achievement and growth gains. However, the data usage priorities focused on state-level generated data. Data on the local level did not necessarily align with state-level data in practicality, objective or use. This has created confusion among schools on how to use data effectively to drive improvement.

Data Utilization Assumptions

The Learning Evaluation process proposed here makes certain assumptions about how data will be gathered, regarded and used.

- Multiple sources of data: data is collected, created, consulted, analyzed and prioritized based on the goals and objectives of the school: quantitative, qualitative and anecdotal evidence is consulted. In essence, teacher teams become hubs of action research.

- Teams collectively interpret evidence: data is created, collected and presented to teams for analysis.

- Pedagogical practices are associated with data: data is used to critically examine instructional practices.

Case Study: With the Right Information, Teachers Flourish

The math department at Aboite High School had experienced some recent turnover and the state standards for high-school math had gone through a rigorous restructuring at the state level. The requirements for high school graduation had also changed, leaving Aboite's curriculum, scope and sequence and course progressions outdated and out of compliance with the new requirements. Mr. Lillard's collaborative skills would be put to the test navigating the changes.

Mr. Lillard started with a small-scale qualitative study of the stakeholders, in this case the principal, three assistant principals and the teachers (certified math instructors). The focus of the work was teacher evaluation.

During qualitative data-gathering he learned about these stakeholders' beliefs, perspectives, values, wanted changes and desired status quo. Using that data, the team was able to build a system that could be agreed upon by the administration and the teachers. They had a process-oriented document that emphasized their needs. Using the Learning Evaluation as a guiding tool, they constructed new elements that were site-specific. It was a broad document that emphasized discussion and conversation over quantitative data.

Aboite High School believed that their use of quantitative data was more than proficient, but felt they lacked collaborative discussions about data at the school, classroom and individual student level. The rubric reflected that, as a tool not to document success or failure, but to communicate, strategize, plan action and implement it. From the broad constructs in the Learning Evaluation document they were able to create a multi-tiered system of support that worked in inter-disciplinary teams, relying less on quantitative data, to identify students requiring intervention. They used the qualitative data appropriately and worked in collaborative teams to identify root cause and tailored instruction for students. The quantitative data told them who needed help; it was the team using their knowledge that discussed, debated, chose and administered the interventions. A teacher that was able to successfully contribute to that initiative through that process would be successful in his or her evaluation. Again, this was all done to meet a local need. Each district, school, staff and team has its own needs to improve adult and student learning. The processes outlined in this new evaluation should help teams identify those needs and incorporate elementals as necessary.

Goal Setting

Teachers and school teams establish performance goals for themselves and their students. Teachers facilitate student achievement goals through a positive, collaborative relationship with their students. Students drive the implementation of performance goals facilitated by the teacher. goals. The establishment of all goals is based off data utilization and collaborative processes.

The creation of goals is a product of collaborative processes. Goals are a shared experience, even if the goal relates to an individual teacher or individual student. The goals are collectively developed and shared by all members of the school community. Achievement of goals is the result of teamwork.

Goal Setting Assumptions

- Goal facilitation: teachers facilitate goal-setting with students. Teachers create goals as a result of collaboration.

131

- Goals—for teachers and students—result from collaborative processes and data utilization.
- Goals drive actions through collective responsibility.
- Goals established are assumed to have been created through data utilization and collaborative processes to build consensus through shared governance.

Case Study: Vision Starts with Knowing What Your Target Is…

At Park Center Middle School, transitioning students from fifth grade to sixth grade and establishing a solid foundation of learning targets has been a challenge. Mrs. Schraughben, the school principal, was up to the task. She had a group of dedicated teachers who simply needed a target to visualize.

During weekly collaboration Mrs. Schraughben and the sixth-grade team were reviewing the students' data from their fifth-grade year at the local elementary schools. They were going over the data, looking for trends and student strengths and weaknesses. Mr. Summers, a sixth-grade teacher, made a comment when they were looking at the English language arts data: "Seventy-five percent of the kids look like they're proficient in English language arts coming from the local elementary schools." He also noted that this was his eighth year in teaching, and that this was the eighth year in a row that around three-fourths of the incoming students had been proficient. Mr. Summers stated that he wanted to set a different goal for the students this year, in addition to the regular student achievement goals based on standardized test scores. Thinking back on his past experiences he commented that sixth graders transitioning from elementary school always seemed to lack the executive functions and executive skills necessary to be successful in middle school. Mr. Summers' idea was to use anecdotal data and observation data to identify students who were struggling with organizing themselves for five teachers, instead of just one. Mr. Summers set a goal for the team to teach all sixth graders the necessary skills together, observe students over a period of two weeks, and then refer those who were struggling to an intervention group to teach the skills. The team and principal loved the idea.

Mrs. Schraughben grabbed a marker and started taking notes on chart paper, eliciting ideas from the team about the skills that students needed to be successful in middle school. The team compiled a list of eight skills students needed to be successful at Park Center. Mrs. Schraughben created a simple referral form for teachers to use that identified the skills and an individual student's strengths and weaknesses. The teachers developed a series of short lessons to teach every sixth grader. After the teachers had the students in class and were able to observe them and develop a relationship with them, those who needed it could be referred to an intervention group to explicitly teach them the agreed-upon skills.

After the first quarter 90 sixth graders out of 230 had received the additional instruction in executive skills. The teachers celebrated in their collaboration meeting to start the third quarter, because based on their observations students were learning the executive functions. At the end of the year student formative and summative assessment data showed an increase in proficiency from the year before for this cohort of students. Overall, students grew in achievement from fifth to sixth grade in all subjects. This had never happened at Park Center before. Usually, there was a slight dip in achievement from fifth to sixth grade. Not this year, thanks to great collaboration and goal setting, focused on things that have the most profound impact.

Curriculum and Pedagogy

What we teach and how we teach it is the realization of a Learning Evaluation. Hence the importance of the Student-Centered Observation constructs, as outlined in the rubric. The curriculum and pedagogical practices of the school are a result of the collaborative team's ability to synthesize information, plan action, attempt interventions, examine their practice and change to develop and implement the best instructional practices for their team or school.

Curriculum and Pedagogy Assumptions

- Teachers work as a team to clarify essential learning for students.
- Teachers create learning guides and scaffold content and practices to increase student growth and learning.
- Teachers work together to identify best practices, try, fail, try again and succeed.
- Teachers formally and informally assess and discuss the results of their work to plan, intervene and change instructional practices.

Case Study: We Can't Do What We Have Always Done

Mr. Allen had been dealt a fairly good hand as a first-year principal. His staff at Eastside Elementary was full of expert reading teachers. With recent budget cuts, he had to redesign the school's reading program. Change had been needed at Eastside for years. The reading program needed to be restructured.

Mr. Allen was able to find a few key contributors to the staff, teacher leaders who saw the need for change but had never been able to fully realize its movement. Mrs. Smith, a well-respected teacher on staff, was able to convince enough teachers that change was needed in reading. Most teachers could see the need for a restructured approach to reading. Mr. Allen could sense that the teachers were more worried about having something done to them in terms of what or how they taught than they were about change itself. They wanted to have a voice and influence over the reading change.

Using the learning evaluation as a guide, the leadership team at the school was able to consult reading research and develop a progression of reading skills and abilities from Kindergarten through fifth grade. Impactful contributors collaboratively established and clarified essential learning.

The entire school used the literacy learning progressions to plan lessons, implement programs, develop formative assessments and use data to meet student reading needs.

Improvement and Examination of Practice

Teachers need a safe place to examine their practice in order to improve. The safer the environment, the more professional the interactions amongst teachers and between teachers and administrators, the more likely teachers are to improve and by extension improve student learning and growth. But teachers have to be willing to try new methods, strategies and approaches to teaching and learning (Donohoo, 2017). They also have to have no fear of the consequences for becoming vulnerable. Teachers need the autonomy to give their kids autonomy. However, they need not *individual* but *collective* autonomy. Teacher teams need the freedom to try and fail together, to not always get it right or feel like they have to be perceived as getting it right all the time. They need collective freedom to practice. Improvement of practice assumes that one is always learning from failures, leading ultimately to success.

Improvement of Practice Assumptions

- Share strengths and weaknesses.
- Maximize each other's strengths and minimize each other's weaknesses.
- Use the team as an avenue to improve on weaknesses and implement strengths.
- Teamwork leads to improved individual and collective performance.
- Learn from each other's successes and failures.
- Drive fear out of the organization.

Case Study: Who Are Your Experts And Do They Have the Freedom And Influence To Make An Impact?

The best teachers did not have a voice at West Side High School. Mrs. James, the principal, knew she had to tap into the experts in the building to strengthen her departments. Mrs. James had in the past used the Teacher Learning Team Cycle from Stephanie Hirsch and Tracy Crow of "Learning Forward" in *Becoming a Learning Team* (2017). She was especially interested in the "Learn individually and collaboratively cycle" for use within the West Side academic departments.

Mrs. James started the year by engaging her department leads in the learning cycle. She led the department heads through the cycle for the first semester, thinking about the overall needs of the school, students and adults. Once the teacher leaders felt comfortable with the process, they were excited to take it back to their departments and begin the work of identifying student and adult needs and building learning agendas for both.

Through the work in the learning cycle the school was able to compile a list of student needs for every subject and the adult professional learning that would have to take place for them to accomplish their goals. The staff had never explored intentionally looking at data to identify student needs. Therefore, they needed a structured protocol for collecting the data, analyzing the data and planning action. The learning cycle was used as a guide to create collaboration protocols. The teams used those protocols to influence structured conversations, creation of new knowledge and action planning.

Needless to say, the end of the year and the start of the next year were exciting times for the staff at West Side High. Teachers were learning new skills and improving their classroom instruction in the process. Drawing on each other's strengths, learning from each other's failures, West Side High had their best graduation rate in years.

Examination of Practice

Teachers observe each other teach and provide feedback. It really is that simple. Too often schools get bogged down with protocols and formals techniques to brainstorm. If teachers would spend more time just having conversations about teaching and learning they would be better off than trying to fit everything they discuss into a framework, protocol or cycle. Let the teachers talk. Teacher-led observation of instructional practices is an assumed practice of a Learning Evaluation. It is a process that is critical to the success of the staff and school. Teachers need time to observe each other teach and provide feedback to one another in a safe, open environment. Feedback amongst teachers is a foundational action that makes them professionals. It is critical that teachers be able to observe, provide feedback, examine their practices and adapt.

Examination of Practice Assumptions

- Teachers observing teachers is a normal professional practice.
- Teachers formally and informally provide feedback to one another.
- Teachers assist each other in progress monitoring, becoming thinking partners.
- Reflection is a collaborative effort.
- Action planning does not happen in isolation.

Case Study: We Must Drive Fear Out of This School

Mrs. Jones, a principal, had a great instructional coach, Mrs. Phillips. They both agreed that the school was proficient in all of the domains in the Learning Evaluation except for "Examination of Practice." They had to create the time for teachers to observe one another teaching and provide each other feedback, without any interference from a coach or administrator. Mrs. Jones redesigned the master schedule and recruited volunteers to observe each other teaching using the Student-Centered Observation Rubric as a guide. The teacher volunteers then reported their experience to the staff, helping to ease any worry or misgivings regarding the observation protocol.

By the end of the first semester all teachers were observing each other and providing informal, formative feedback to one another. Several teachers even commented that their love of teaching had never been stronger because they were able to fail without fear, receive feedback from a peer and try new things. The morale in the building by the end of the year was at an all-time high.

Teacher Influence

Through focusing on data utilization, curriculum and pedagogy, teachers are freed to improve and examine their practice and contribute to each other's success. The processes are developed at the local level. Teachers decide through consensus and cohesion the best methods to employ through the use of a Learning Evaluation. Notice that in these documents the only items that are implemented by the teachers are collaborative processes. All other strategies, methods, programs, philosophies and tactics are decided on by the teams through processes in the evaluation. Teachers need to have familiar knowledge about each other's practice. If knowledge about one another's work develops via learning together collaboratively, and a learning stance is assumed, then teachers co-construct knowledge about effective teaching practices.

Knowing each other's practice builds cohesion. The principal's role in all of this is to facilitate the conversation, steer consensus and hold teams accountable for the collaborative decisions that they make. Accountability is redefined. Accountability currently lends itself to meaning something related to letter grades, test scores, evaluation ratings and rankings. Accountability in this model means being responsible to the collective decisions made by the team, regardless of any quantifiable outcome. Teamwork and agreed-upon actions are placed first, analysis of results second. The theory is that if the teams follow the process, they will have success more often than failure, with a variety of initiatives, programs and strategies impacting students' learning in the long run. We need to hold each other accountable to the process, not the end result, because the results have to be owned by everyone. The end result simply communicates a need, or next step. It does not communicate overall success. Overall success is found in the foundational work of the team(s). This requires leaders responsive to teacher collaboration. Teachers must be empowered and have direct involvement in decision making. This creates an environment where teams can create and share knowledge.

Subjectivity Is A Good Thing

All performance appraisals are subjective. There is actually no way around the subjectivity of assessing performance. Subjectivity is a good thing. In the case of schools, if a Learning Evaluation is employed and a shared meaning and understanding is the driver of the evaluation, bias can actually decrease because of the shared knowledge, understanding, assumptions and expectations. Regardless, eliminating subjectivity from performance appraisals is impossible. As soon as educators realize that they are stuck with the subjective nature of judging another human's performance, we can move on and create a system that is shared and embraced by all.

First Things First

The Learning Evaluation is flexible and adaptable, and educators must be ready and willing to use the learning evaluation as a starting point with the intention of changing it to meet the local context of the school. Not all schools have the same needs, set the same goals or try to invoke the same strategies to improve. The Learning Evaluation Rubric is a living document. The document is founded in learning organization principles linked to PLC processes for education. The constructs and their underlying assumptions are the foundation of a learning evaluation, not the end. Schools may wish to emphasize, deemphasize, remove or add components that are applicable to them, their goals, objectives and data analysis. Teachers create rubrics for students, just as educational leaders create rubrics for themselves. This is a subjective document highlighting broad constructs to assess a teacher's ability to contribute to a professional learning community as a learner. The narrower details of how that work gets done must be decided at the local level.

Case Study: Implementing A Learning Evaluation

A New Challenge

Mr. Schultz was a veteran principal of eight years, now starting his ninth year in a new district. This was an exciting time for Mr. Schultz, because— although he had found success during his previous eight years at the same school and had a great relationship with his teaching staff—he was ready for a new challenge. An elementary school in a neighboring county had a principal opening. North Star Elementary School had been regarded as one of the best elementary schools in the area for a number of years. Two years ago, the principle of 12 years and a number of veteran staff members had retired: since then the school had struggled to maintain its success in standardized test scores, perception in the community and satisfaction among parents. Mr. Schultz had a professional relationship with the superintendent of the district and was blown away by the innovative things they were doing at the district level because of their commitment to be a learning organization. North Star needed a leader that could facilitate the improvement of the school through collaborative processes. The district already had systems in place to help schools be successful. North Star needed a leader that could tap into the talent and expertise of the staff. After Mr. Schultz's interview with the superintendent, they both agreed that he would be the collaborative leader North Star needed to be the learning community it once was and could be again.

A Solid Foundation

Mr. Schultz learned very quickly that North Star had a solid foundation for improvement. Teachers believed that they could have a positive effect on student achievement. They had the desire to help all students learn. They had great teachers; teachers with superb individual talent. They even had the Learning Evaluation system that the superintendent had shown him during the interview. In that interview the superintendent had emphasized how the learning evaluation system provided school leaders with broad constructs to guide teachers in the improvement of their school. Upon review of the Learning Evaluation, Mr. Schultz realized that it was not what he had expected. Even though the documents were easy to read, follow and understand, he had not expected that there would be so much variability to influence the choice and implementation of programing to move the school forward. Mr. Schultz was excited about the freedom to facilitate teacher teams, but also very nervous. The school could not sit back and wait for someone to tell them what to do. They actually had to make some informed decisions and try.

Mr. Schultz was a great leader. He was collaborative and motivating. Teachers trusted him and respected his expertise and ability to listen. But, in the district he had come from, program development and creation was not part of the job description. Mr. Schultz's strength was in taking what was handed down to him as a principal and his staff, interpreting it, linking it to current needs and working within constrictive frameworks to improve. Actually, using a Learning Evaluation to improve a school was a scary and new thought process for Mr. Schultz. But, this was what he had wanted: a challenge.

Mr. Schultz addressed his staff at the beginning of the year. After all of the formal legalities and logistical processes had been discussed and laid out, Mr. Schultz took the Learning Evaluation document and asked the staff to consider one question, "What does this look like at North Star Elementary?" He asked them to ask themselves the same question for each domain. "What does this look like at North Star Elementary for data utilization, goal setting......?

That question was at the heart of their collaboration meetings for the entire year. In practice, North Star was able to identify the processes for each domain of the Learning Evaluation that they chartered, created, changed and adapted together. By agreeing upon the process to make the rubric come to life, bias was reduced, teachers had influence and ownership of the processes and the tools were used to advance professional and student learning.

Learning Evaluation Rubric Assumptions: Graphic

The Learning Evaluation Rubric Assumptions

New assumptions play out in the Learning Evaluation Rubric, grounded in its vision: to establish a teacher evaluation model that incorporates the greatest factors influencing student achievements as the primary method to evaluate teacher performance. These are collective efficacy, collaboration and professional learning.

Each process embedded in the Learning Evaluation entails its own assumptions, set out in the Broad Assumptions of Teacher Efficacy in Figure 6.7.

Collaborative Teams Assumptions

- Teachers in a learning evaluation assume certain aspects of collaboration
- They value input from one another
- They collectively solve problems
- They support one another
- They influence professional learning
- They share decision making
- They find, use and share resources
- They cultivate ideas, creativity and innovation

Data Utilization Assumptions

- Multiple sources of data: data is collected, created, consulted, analyzed and prioritized based on the goals and objectives of the school. Quantitative, qualitative and anecdotal evidence is consulted. Teacher teams become hubs of action research.
- Teams collectively interpret evidence: data is created, collected and presented to teams for analysis.
- Pedagogical practices are associated with data: data is used to critically examine instructional practices.

Goal Setting Assumptions

- Goal facilitation: teachers facilitate goal setting with students. Student-created goals are a result of collaboration between the students and the teacher.
- Teacher and student goals result from collaborative processes and data utilization.
- Goals drive actions through collective responsibility
- Goals established, are assumed to have been created through data utilization and collaborative processes to build consensus through shared governance

Curriculum and Pedagogy Assumptions

- Teachers work as a team to clarify essential learning for students
- Teachers create learning guides and scaffold content and practices to increase student growth and learning
- Teachers work together to identify best practices, try, fail, try again and succeed.
- Teachers formally and informally assess and discuss the results of their work to plan, intervene and change instructional practices

Improvement of Practice Assumptions

- Share strengths and weaknesses
- Maximize each other's strengths and minimize each other's weaknesses
- Use the team as an avenue to improve weaknesses and implement strengths
- Teamwork leads to improved individual and collective performance
- Learn from each other's successes and failures
- Drive fear out of the organization

Examination of Practices Assumptions

- Teachers observing teachers is a normal professional practice
- Teachers formally and informally provide feedback to one another
- Teachers assist each other in progress monitoring, becoming think partners
- Reflection is a collaborative effort
- Action planning does not happen in isolation

Figure 6.6 Learning Evaluation rubric assumptions: guide

Learning Assumptions Concept Flow

Broad Assumptions of Teacher Efficacy	
Motivation	Teachers are intrinsically motivated to help students
Teamwork	Educators solve problems with teamwork
Collective Efficacy	Educators are interdependently linked to the success of the organization
Context	The local school culture, community needs, institutional knowledge and cultural proficiency are prioritized in the organizational objectives and goals
Collective Inquiry	Educators have processes that influence critical examination of practice
Collaboration	Educators strategize root causes and intervene to meet goals and objectives

Impactful Assumptions
School are unique entities. Best practices from other domains are consulted, but not blindly adopted.
Principals facilitate and lead teacher teams as the most effective way to assess teacher effectiveness.
Teachers demonstrate their effectiveness by being an active member of a Professional Learning Community.
Teacher evaluation rubrics focus on processes of collective inquiry, collaboration, and context.
Teachers work within collaborative teams to assess their needs as professionals, and the needs of their students. Educators collectively research, prioritize, select and implement strategies to improve professional learning and student learning, demonstrating their effectiveness.
Communicate, Communicate, Communicate

New Processes of Evaluation
Student Learning Focused Mission
Contributions to Collaborative Teams
Data Utilization
Goal Setting
Curriculum and Pedagogy
Improvement of Practice
Examination of Practice

Figure 6.7 Learning assumptions concept flow

References

Donohoo, J. (2017). *Collective efficacy: How educators' beliefs impact student learning*. Thousand Oaks, CA: Corwin.

Donohoo, J., Hattie, J., & Eells, R. (2018, March). The power of collective efficacy. *Educational Leadership, 75*(6), 40–44.

Goddard, R., Goddard, Y., Kim, E. S., & Miller, R. (2015). A theoretical and empirical analysis of the roles of instructional leadership, teacher collaboration, and collective efficacy beliefs in support of student learning. *American Journal of Education, 121*(4), 501–530.

Hirsch, S., & Crow, T. (2017). *Becoming a learning team*. Oxford, OH: Learning Forward.

Jones, N. D., Bettini, E., & Brownell, M. (2019). Competing strands of educational reform policy: Can collaborative school reform and teacher evaluation reform be reconciled? *The Elementary School Journal, 119*(3), 468–486.

Moss, C. M., & Brookhart, S. M. (2012). Learning targets: helping students aim for understanding in today's lesson. Alexandria, VA: ASCD.

Sergiovanni, T., & Starratt, R. (2007). *Supervision: A redefinition*. New York, NY: McGraw-Hill Education.

Supplemental Material

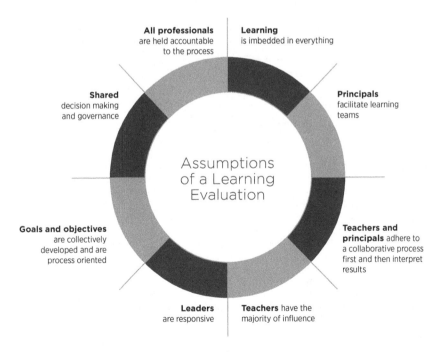

Figure 6.8 Assumptions of a Learning Evaluation

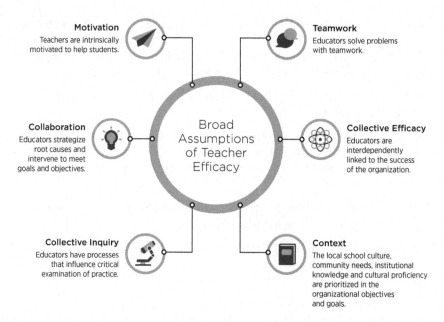

Figure 6.9 Broad assumptions of teacher efficacy

Paramount Assumption:
The mission of the school is to ensure that all students learn, grow and achieve academically and behaviorally. Student learning is paramount. We live and embrace this assumption by learning as adults through a process of collective inquiry.

Figure 6.10 Paramount assumption

Professional Learning Communities

PLCs are groups or teams of educators committed to collaborating and being engaged in collective inquiry into best practices and current performance in an environment that supports relevant research. The PLC strives to gather evidence of current learning, develop new strategies and analyze the impact. PLCs take collective responsibility for the results of student achievement and teacher professional learning.

Figure 6.11 Professional learning communities

Mission and Beliefs

All students can learn and learn at high levels. This is the most basic aspect of a PLC. Failure to embrace this mission and belief would be an indication that an individual no longer needs to be a teacher.

Figure 6.12 Mission and beliefs

Professional Learning Communities

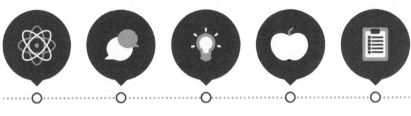

| Teachers use data to identify instructional strategies in order to increase student learning and achievement. | Teachers work in PLCs to observe one another teaching, provide feedback and improve their practice. | Teachers recognize and celebrate each other's strengths. | Teachers analyze student work and investigate ways to provide more rigorous instruction and push student learning. | Teachers identify areas of improvement and work as a team to help each other become better at their practice. |

Figure 6.13 Professional learning communities: graphic

Contributions to Learning and Knowledge

Teachers contribute to learning new knowledge by receiving and providing feedback on their practice to and from one another.

Teachers discuss and try new and research-based instructional strategies; reading current trends, research, publications and innovative practices from other teachers and experts.

Teachers and administrators work collaboratively to establish class/subject and individual goals of student achievement and develop action plans to meet those goals.

Action plans incorporate resources needed, professional learning and intermittent time frames for assessing the success of the student learning goals.

Teachers work in collaboration to deliver a guaranteed and viable curriculum. Teachers analyze state standards to clarify essential learning and the depth of knowledge students need to learn, grow and achieve academically.

Teachers develop and use assessments to pace student learning, analyze data and identify students in need of enrichment or remediation.

Figure 6.14 Contributions to learning and knowledge